FIRESIDE

By Nancy Berezin

The Gentle Birth Book: A Practical
Guide to Leboyer Family-Centered Delivery

After a Loss in Pregnancy

Help for Families Affected by a Miscarriage, a Stillbirth, or the Loss of a Newborn

NANCY BEREZIN

Introduction by Jan Schneider, M.D.

A FIRESIDE BOOK
Published by Simon and Schuster
New York

Library of Congress Cataloging in Publication Data
Berezin, Nancy, date.
After a loss in pregnancy.
"A Fireside book."
Bibliography: p.
Includes index.
1. Perinatal mortality—Psychological aspects.
2. Miscarriage—Psychological aspects. 3. Bereavement.
I. Title.
RG631.B47   155.9'37   81-18438
AACR2
ISBN 0-671-25525-8

Grateful acknowledgment is extended to the following publishers and journals for permission to reprint copyrighted materials:

Holt, Rinehart and Winston, Publishers, for "Home Burial" from *The Poetry of Robert Frost*, edited by Edward Connery Lathem. Copyright 1930, 1939, © 1969 by Holt, Rinehart and Winston. Copyright © 1958 by Robert Frost. Copyright © 1967 by Lesley Frost Ballantine.

Little, Brown and Company for "After great pain, a formal feeling comes" from *The Complete Poems of Emily Dickinson*, edited by Thomas H. Johnson, Copyright 1929 by Martin Dickinson Bianchi; © renewed 1957 by Mary L. Hampson.

The American Journal of Nursing for "Books to Help Children Understand Death" by Gretchen Curtis Mills, R.N., Copyright © 1979, American Journal of Nursing Company.

The Journal of Pastoral Care for "Prayer Upon the Death of an Infant," by John Gordon Anderson, Copyrighted by the Association for Clinical Pastoral Education, Inc.

Mothering Publications, Inc., for the following poems by Marion Cohen, © Mothering Publications, Inc., P.O. Box 2046, Albuquerque, NM 87103: "The One Who Died," "Intensive Care Nursery II," "Trying to Conceive Poem 4," and a portion of "Fourth Pregnancy."

Acknowledgments

SO MANY PEOPLE contributed to the preparation of this book—parents and health professionals who opened their hearts and lent their expertise—you know who you are and I thank you all. In addition, I would like to thank my talented editor, Catherine Shaw, for her continuing faith in me; Alice Campbell, my friend and manuscript typist; Jan Schneider, M.D., for his wise and thoughtful manuscript review; and my wonderful family, who maintained their cheerfulness in the face of the endless piles of tape transcriptions and journal clippings which were the foundations of this project.

For new beginnings

Contents

9

Introduction:
An
Obstetrician's View

THROUGHOUT HISTORY pregnancy has demanded its toll of the mother, her unborn child, and newborn baby. It seems incredible that just eighty years ago in this country, for every hundred deliveries one mother died and ten babies did not survive to their first birthday. This century has seen dramatic progress in the reduction of mortality: risk of maternal death is now one one-hundredth of what it was in 1900 and infant mortality is one-tenth of the rate at that time. Falling rates, however, can bring little solace to the mother whose baby dies and thus becomes a statistic. Indeed, the grief of such women today may be greater than in a bygone era, when the frequency of death must have had at least some effect in lessening its impact.

In her book, Nancy Berezin analyzes with great sensitivity the many issues that surround unsuccessful pregnancy. Her inclusion of early pregnancy loss is of particular interest, since spontaneous abortion has frequently been assumed to carry little emotional impact. Many miscarriages are known to be caused by chromosomal abnormalities incompatible with life and medicine has tended to consider miscarriage as a pregnancy that never was. Yet, to the mother, it represents a baby who will never be. This undoubtedly is one area in which there has been poor communication between health professionals and the patient, with inadequate consideration of the grief felt by the mother.

It struck this obstetrician as remarkable how rarely the women

11

interviewed by Ms. Berezin seemed to have turned to their physicians for solace. The obstetrician is rarely identified as a source of support and comfort. In practice, one sees many examples of patients who reject their former physician and turn to another when they become pregnant again after an unsuccessful pregnancy. Superstition, guilt, anger, shame, unpleasant memories, and disappointment must all feature in such a rejection.

Traditionally, the medical profession has not dealt well with the grief-stricken patient. Perhaps the obstetrician, in what is generally considered to be a happy specialty, is even less well prepared than are others to adequately console a patient at a time of great sorrow. The dialogue between a distraught patient and her physician is often artificial and strained. In part to mask the anguish of failure, the physician tends to respond tearlessly in a manner he perceives as professional. The stiff upper lip becomes a mask. At the same time, the mother in her sorrow and confusion may attempt to disguise her anger and substitute the courageous posture she believes is expected of a patient. When the "physician mask" talks to the "patient mask," neither communicates honestly with the other.

There is no obstetrician who has not strained through a stethoscope to catch only the sickening silence of an absent fetal heartbeat. Common sense and compassion tell him that his facial expression must not betray his anxiety. He tells himself that surely the heartbeat is somewhere . . . it's just hiding . . . I must not scare the patient. Of course, today there are reliable means of confirming or disproving the diagnosis, but that first episode with a stethoscope is the most emotionally wrenching. Somehow, one must gently warn or prepare the woman for what she already suspects—that something is amiss. Such communications often become confused. I remember being compelled to tell one very special patient that her baby had died in utero. That evening she telephoned me in tears, apologizing over and over. When I asked why she felt she needed to apologize, she repeated her memory of our conversation, which was that I had told her that she had never been pregnant in the first place. Concerned, I repeated again what I thought I had said that morning. Her response was: "But then why were you so angry?" What I had assumed to be the demeanor of professionalism had been distorted into a facial expression of anger. I should have cried, but I did not. Some years later, when her subsequent baby was delivered by one of my colleagues—to whom she had turned in her rejection of me—I cried inside once again.

It is clear that patients whose pregnancies are lost, whether by early abortion, fetal death, or the death of a newborn baby, require much greater support than we as physicians have given in the past. Although grief has come under scientific scrutiny and the mourning process has been classified and analyzed, every patient bears a unique and individual sorrow. Time may modify the pain and the grief, but to some extent the scar will remain forever. The scar may be great or small; as obstetricians, we have the opportunity to offer compassion and help in the earliest phases of the healing process.

—*Jan Schneider, M.D.*
CHAIRMAN, DEPARTMENT OF OBSTETRICS
AND GYNECOLOGY, THE MEDICAL COLLEGE
OF PENNSYLVANIA, PHILADELPHIA

Foreword

SHORTLY AFTER I began writing this book, I received a telephone call from a friend. "Nancy," she said, "my neighbor has just given birth to an anencephalic child who is not expected to live more than a few hours. Her obstetrician told her to go home and pretend it never happened, and to try to get pregnant again as soon as possible. She's very upset and wonders whether that advice is really right for her. Would you call her?"

I did call, with the address of a local clinic that specialized in family crises of this kind, a list of reading material, and what meager words of sympathy I could offer to a woman I had never met, whose grief was shattering, and whose physician had given her what amounted to a prescription for emotional illness.

Why? Because no amount of pretending would ever bring this woman's baby back or convince her he had never existed. The obstetrician—also, incidentally, a woman—had been well-meaning, but her advice was founded on the terrible misconception that grief can be sidestepped, that the joy of a successful second pregnancy could miraculously erase the memory of a loss.

Sadly, no such miracles exist. The work of mourning is indeed accomplished, but only over time. To sidestep it is to risk the more serious consequence that grief will remain unresolved. And conceiving a child to "replace" one who has died does an injustice not only to the parents, who will still be looking backward with regret rather

15

than ahead with anticipation, but even more so to the child. For to spend a lifetime in the shadow of a dead sibling is seldom to spend a very happy or fulfilling life.

There is no single course of action appropriate to the needs of all bereaved parents (and a parent who loses a child in pregnancy, even relatively early in gestation, *is* a bereaved parent). Each heals at his or her own pace in his or her own way. Some couples draw closer together, others are swept so far apart that reconciliation becomes extremely difficult. Whether to visit a counselor or join a support group, stay at home or return to work, what to say to older siblings if there are any, and when to attempt another pregnancy are issues that may take considerable effort to resolve. Frequently, the needs of family members conflict. Everyone is vulnerable. There is *always* blame.

This book was written to offer the experience of couples who have worked through the crisis of a fetal or newborn death, and of the professionals who aided and encouraged them, to those currently confronting that crisis. It offers no magical solutions—only the reminder that others have been there before and know it hurts.

Equally, it was written for the obstetrician who counseled my friend's neighbor and all of the other well-intentioned people who would advise the bereaved to go home and forget.

As the findings of researchers suggest, and the words of the parents themselves confirm, "keeping a stiff upper lip" is a destructive waste of time. The object is not to forget, but to remember . . . and go on.

—Nancy Berezin
Westchester County, N.Y.

1
The Couple's Response

NEVER IN HUMAN HISTORY has the process of childbearing been approached with such justifiable optimism as today in the industrialized nations of the world. And never, when things go wrong, has the impact of an unsuccessful pregnancy so devastated prospective parents.

We take for granted, as part of the natural order of things, that our children should outlive us. Yet it was not so very long ago that Western society regarded deaths in pregnancy and early childhood as predictable and commonplace. No eighteenth- or nineteenth-century parent could expect that every child conceived would be born alive and grow to healthy maturity. On the contrary, prior to the widespread use of sterile surgical techniques and the even more recent discovery of antibiotics, it was generally assumed that a large family might lose up to half of its offspring. Those who survived birth would often succumb to common childhood killers such as infantile diarrhea, pneumonia, diphtheria, and streptococcal infection. The prodigious Johann Sebastian Bach fathered twenty youngsters, of whom only nine lived to reach adulthood.

By its universality, the precariousness of maternal and child health helped to cushion the impact of losses on the survivors. Expectant couples entering the health care system today have no such cushion. In its place, technological leaps during the past century have created a climate of success. The satisfying drop in fetal and newborn

17

mortality has given both obstetrical practitioners and parents cause to emphasize the positive. Victory is always a more pleasant topic than defeat.

Yet defeat still occurs in obstetrics—exactly how frequently, we remain uncertain. But it is now believed that fewer than one out of five conceptuses ever reaches term alive. True, most pregnancies that terminate spontaneously do so relatively early in gestation, but that is hardly assurance that the event will be regarded lightly by the prospective mother. On the contrary, even a single miscarriage may leave emotional scars that last a lifetime. Although beneficial to the species in the long run, natural selection can be merciless in individual cases.

As for the newborn period, it continues to be the most dangerous stage of childhood. In one British survey, the number of deaths prior to labor, during labor, and during the first week of life exceeded by roughly tenfold the number occurring for the remainder of the first year of life. Complications of pregnancy may also have wide-ranging repercussions, so that children who survive the early months may succumb in later years to problems stemming from intrauterine influences. This "continuum of reproductive casualty" is sadly evident in the estimated twenty million persons in the United States born with congenital malformations, cerebral palsy, mental retardation, deafness, blindness, and other neurosensory defects.

Parents bereaved by a fetal or newborn death are continually asking: "Why?" Why couldn't the baby have lived? Why have they, rather than their siblings or friends or the couple down the block, been singled out for misfortune? Why did God . . . or fate . . . or the doctors allow this to happen? That the picture is improving is beyond question. That it is also becoming more complex, so that our very successes tend to increase our frustration and inability to reconcile ourselves to what remains hidden, must also be recognized. For the couple affected by a reproductive casualty, *almost* good enough is never good enough.

Mourning for an unsuccessful pregnancy does not end when the mother is discharged from the hospital. Bereaved parents frequently reckon the period of convalescence, not in hours or days, but in months or years. Yet education of those medical caregivers whose responsibility it is to meet parental needs for referral and counseling has traditionally been sketchy, and community psychosocial support services are woefully inadequate.

In the late 1970s, D. Gary Benfield, M.D., and his co-workers at

The Children's Hospital Medical Center of Akron, Ohio, examined the grief response to newborn death of fifty families referred to the neonatal intensive-care unit. They found that parental grief, although not significantly affected by such variables as birthweight, duration of life, extent of parent-infant contact, previous loss, or parental age, was "often adversely influenced" by attitudes and behavior of family, friends, and hospital personnel.

Clemson University sociologists Larry G. Peppers and Ronald J. Knapp queried one hundred mothers and fathers to determine whether intensity of mourning was substantially related to the gestational age at which the loss occurred. They found no difference in maternal reaction (e.g., sadness, insomnia, guilt feelings) between mothers who had suffered early fetal losses and mothers who had suffered either a stillbirth or a neonatal death. However, the researchers found that the nature and intensity of grief were strongly affected by the inappropriate reactions of friends, relatives, and caregivers.

These and similar recent investigations raise a number of provocative questions. Why do we as a culture, laymen and health professionals alike, respond so poorly to bereavement? What is different about the death of a fetus or infant that makes it especially difficult to lend appropriate support to the parents? And finally, what can be done to strengthen support systems for grieving parents, in the hospital and in the community? In this chapter and the chapters that follow we will examine some of these issues.

A Word About Terminology

To the parent confronting them for the first time, scientific and lay designations for the death of a child in pregnancy appear dishearteningly confused. The general public uses the term "miscarriage" when referring to the expulsion from the womb of a previable fetus (viability being interpreted as beginning around the twentieth week of pregnancy, when the fetus weighs approximately 500 grams or 1 pound) and "stillbirth" thereafter. Physicians prefer the traditional "spontaneous abortion" for losses in early pregnancy—not to be confused with "induced abortion," or abortion resulting from a procedure designed to interrupt the pregnancy—and "fetal death" for losses beyond the twentieth week. Fetal deaths are further subdivided into those which occur prior to initiation of labor (antepartum) and those occurring during labor and delivery (intrapartum). "Neonatal" or newborn death is defined as the death of a liveborn infant at any time during the first twenty-eight extrauterine days.

Often, fetal and neonatal deaths are combined for statistical purposes under the broader heading of "perinatal death," which in the United States encompasses all losses occurring between the twentieth week of gestation and the twenty-eighth day of human life. In Britain and the rest of Europe, however, the term "perinatal death" refers only to those losses which occur between twenty-eight weeks of gestation and the seventh day of neonatal life.*

To complicate matters further, reporting of casualties within the United States differs from state to state and community to community. In most states, the law implies or specifically orders that all liveborn products of conception be registered as births, and an appropriate certificate filed with the local health department. In fact, few hospitals would consider a fetus weighing 80 or 100 grams a child, although the heart may be beating at birth. State guidelines for stillbirth tend to be more consistently followed, with hospitals reporting only fetuses beyond a certain gestational age—say, seven months—as births, and the rest considered spontaneous abortions. Many hospitals informally apply this rule to live as well as stillborn fetuses; others set an arbitrary weight limit, electing not to report fetuses weighing under 500, 1000, or 1500 grams, as the case may be.

In a measure designed to standardize the international reporting of reproductive casualties, the World Health Organization in 1950 recommended that use of the term "abortion" be entirely discontinued and all fetal and newborn deaths reported according to four subclassifications: (1) early fetal losses of less than twenty weeks gestation; (2) twenty to twenty-eight weeks gestation; (3) over twenty-eight weeks gestation; and (4) unknown gestational age. Although a step forward, this method, too, has been found wanting by at least one group of investigators, who point out that spontaneous abortions in which no preservable embryonic material is found are excluded from all four categories.

---

* The fact that fetal deaths between the twentieth and twenty-eighth week of gestation and newborn deaths occurring beyond the first week of life are not reported as perinatal losses *except* in the United States undoubtedly contributes to the continuing discrepancy between U.S. perinatal mortality statistics and those of Sweden and other industrialized nations. For discussion of other factors involved—especially, variations in the distribution and utilization of maternity health care—see Chapter 7.

It is hoped that someday parents and health care professionals will be able to communicate on common linguistic ground. Certainly, uniform designations are needed if we are to make any legitimate comparisons between local figures, or establish the relative importance of various contributing conditions to the worldwide incidence of reproductive casualty.

UNSUCCESSFUL PREGNANCY AS A SITUATIONAL CRISIS

A dramatic change in the major circumstances of a person's life can provoke what is known as a situational crisis—a state of emergency characterized by unusual psychological stress. Among the common causes of situational crises are: marital separation or divorce, a severe accident or crippling illness, alcoholism or drug addiction in the family, sexual molestation, or victimization by a crime or disaster. Heading the list, according to Gilbert Kliman, M.D., founder of The Center for Preventive Psychiatry in White Plains, New York, is bereavement.

"We know that bereaved families have a higher incidence of mental and psychosomatic illness than the general population," reports Dr. Kliman. "Loss of a loved person is often a long-enduring pathogenic influence."

For the woman who experiences a fetal or neonatal death, this loss occurs when she is at her most vulnerable, both physically and psychologically. Physically, she may be weakened by blood loss following spontaneous abortion or exhausted from the strain of labor and delivery—and numbed by medication, in either case. Following a stillbirth or a newborn death she is likely to be subject to discomfort from an episiotomy or abdominal stitches as well as the painful reminder of her swollen, milky breasts.

Psychologically, in addition to the multiple disappointments and disillusionments involved in a loss of such magnitude, she may face an array of "minor failures," such as her inability to follow Lamaze-prepared childbirth techniques. She is, furthermore, still involved in the altered emotional state of pregnancy, with its rapid shifts of mood, fantasies, crying spells, and sudden attacks of anxiety.

Dr. Gerald Caplan, who under the auspices of Harvard Medical School's Laboratory of Community Psychiatry was responsible for

Frequency and Comparison of Parent Grief Responses*

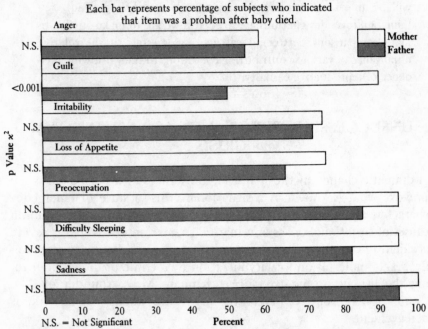

Each bar represents percentage of subjects who indicated that item was a problem after baby died.

*From J. Cullberg, "Mental Reactions of Women to Perinatal Death," *Psychosomatic Medicine in Obstetrics and Gynaecology*, 3rd International Congress, London 1971, p. 326 (S. Karger AG, Basel, 1972).

much of the original work upon which our understanding of crisis theory rests, felt strongly that pregnancy itself represents a significant challenge, or period of disequilibrium, in a woman's life. A woman's reasons for choosing motherhood, her basic personality structure and methods of solving problems, and the quality of support she receives from her partner and "key helping figures" are all instrumental in determining whether the pregnancy will "lead to greater maturity and healthier relationships or . . . to the kind of pathogenic situation in which the expectant mother prepares to use the coming child as a partial solution for some of her problems." [1]

If the above is true of healthy, successful pregnancies, it should hardly come as a surprise that a tragic outcome places such enormous burdens on the coping skills of both parents.

In the Benfield study, fathers as well as mothers experienced profound emotional reactions to the deaths of their infants. Although the maternal response was generally more intense, in eleven out of fifty couples studied (22 percent) the father's "grief score" exceeded that of his wife.* [2]

In another study, conducted at a Stockholm maternity clinic, J. Cullberg found evidence of serious psychological repercussions in nineteen out of fifty-six women who had experienced perinatal death. Through followup interviews arranged one to two years after the event, the Swedish team found phobias of sterilization and uterine cancer, and obsession with the idea that the rest of the woman's family were going to die, as well as two cases of actual delusional psychosis. Nine bereaved mothers experienced recurrent attacks of acute death anxiety, and twenty-six of the women reported outspoken guilt feelings.[3]

Despite their initially dramatic symptomatology, most of the mothers eventually found it possible to work through their grief and return to normal functioning. However, Cullberg's study underlines the impossibility of setting up a specific timetable for mourning. As one woman phrased it, "Everyone wants to hear that you're coping well, that things are getting better every day. Only it doesn't work out that way. Things do get better, but much more slowly than people are willing to accept."

Although the persistence of serious symptoms beyond six months to a year should suggest that the couple seek out some form of professional crisis intervention, enduring grief responses such as those just described are not uncommon. Perhaps the greatest strain on a woman bereaved by a fetal or newborn death is knowledge that outsiders, even at times her own husband, expect her to react "normally" during a period when a normal reaction to anything is virtually impossible.

"A couple of months after the stillbirth," reported a woman whose previous child had also been stillborn, "I started having anxiety attacks. My lips and hands would go numb, I would shake; I would start hyperventilating. I had never been afraid of death, but I

* The investigators cite several possible explanations for the discrepancy between maternal and paternal responses: First, that men are frequently discouraged by societal pressure from expressing their most intimate feelings; second, that the father of a critically ill newborn is often torn between the demands of home, work, and hospital visits; third, that because responsibility for physician contact and funeral arrangements often rests almost exclusively with the father, he may find it easier to accept the loss, or alternatively, that the lower paternal score reflects a form of denial, and that many fathers would, if tested months or even years afterward, exhibit significantly higher values.

began to think about cancer. I developed migraine headaches. Sometimes, I think that my whole personality changed."

Eleven of the mothers in the Swedish study told of first trying to suppress or deny their feelings, having been advised by hospital staff members or relatives to "pull themselves together," "be brave," or "think about something else." Cullberg notes that in this group of women, the period of mental symptomatology lasted noticeably *longer* than in the mothers who felt free to mourn.[4]

One of the characteristic features of bereavement is the sense of having been singled out for punishment. Mourning is a lonely process, and a woman may feel (with some justification) that nobody, except perhaps another bereaved mother, can really comprehend the depth of her pain and loss. Because, as we shall see, the father's response is typically quite different, it is critical that both partners be alert for trouble spots and seek help before it is too late. After all, an important mutual goal—the birth of this particular child—will never be realized. Considerable psychological effort will have to be expended before each parent reaches the stage of acceptance. During this period of heightened emotional vulnerability, conflicts dating back to childhood or to former marriages in which the current spouse had no part may reappear under a different guise.

If older siblings are involved, their needs will often conflict with the parents' desire for introspection. How these problems are dealt with and how the loss itself is explained, not only to surviving youngsters but to children as yet unborn, may have profound implications for the mental health of the next generation.

If the couple are able to approach the crisis of an unsuccessful pregnancy in a mutually supportive manner; if they are flexible enough to allow necessary alterations in household routines, work schedules, and social life; and particularly if they receive a degree of community support and sensitive treatment in the hands of medical personnel and other caregivers, it is likely that they will emerge from the experience as stronger individuals, and the partnership will endure.

If, on the other hand, the conditions are unfavorable for healthy resolution of grief, then a negative outcome—in the form of separation or divorce, psychosomatic illness, continued emotional disturbance or other pathology—cannot be ruled out.

British psychiatrist Colin Murray Parkes has suggested a list of determinants of the psychological outcome of any bereavement.[5] It might be useful, as we proceed in our discussion of the relationship between prospective parents and the unborn child and the role of societal factors in providing appropriate outlets for grief, to occasionally glance back at Dr. Parkes's list, as a reminder of the multiple obstacles parents face in mourning this very special loss.

Determinants of the Outcome of Bereavement

ANTECEDENT

Childhood experiences (especially losses of significant persons)
Later experiences (especially losses of significant persons)
Previous mental illness (especially depressive illness)
Life crises prior to the bereavement
Relationship with the deceased
    Kinship (spouse, child, parent, etc.)
    Strength of attachment
    Security of attachment
    Degree of reliance
    Intensity of ambivalence (love/hate)
Mode of death
    Timeliness
    Previous warnings
    Preparation for bereavement
    Need to hide feelings

CONCURRENT

Sex
Age
Personality
    Grief proneness
    Inhibition of feelings
Socioeconomic status (social class)
Nationality
Religion (faith and rituals)
Cultural and familial factors influencing expression of grief

SUBSEQUENT

Social support or isolation
Secondary stresses
Emergent life opportunities (options open)

CONFRONTING THE DEATH OF HOPE

"As soon as the diagnosis of pregnancy is made, the expectant mother begins to build up hopes and expectations," says Boston obstetrician

Andrew Elia. "This sudden manifestation of fertility stimulates her thinking, colors her mental imagery and ushers in an era of good will." [6]

Although feelings of ambivalence may recur, on and off, throughout pregnancy, by the middle of the second trimester most women are eagerly fantasizing about the baby's sex, asking themselves whom it will resemble, and following its progress by means of photographs in textbooks and parents' manuals. Prospective fathers, too, may spend considerable time fantasizing about the baby. Although the prospective father is not directly involved in the momentous hormonal and metabolic changes that prepare a woman's body for giving birth, he too has dreams of the future that may heavily involve parenthood. For both partners, the growing fetus comes to represent, not only a person-to-be who will require their love and nurturing, but also evidence of fertility and the embodiment of their aspirations toward immortality.

To demonstrate the existence of strong affectional ties even before birth, pediatrician John H. Kennell and associates at Case Western Reserve School of Medicine examined the grief responses of twenty mothers whose newborns had died in the intensive-care nursery. Clearly identifiable mourning was observed in all of the women studied, regardless of their infant's weight and viability or whether the pregnancy had been planned or unplanned.

Dr. Emanuel Lewis of London's Tavistock Clinic notes that evidence from studies of young widows suggests that it is the loss of a future with their husbands which is particularly painful. "With stillbirth or neonatal death," says Lewis, "it is partly the loss of what might have been, the loss of experience in the future, which makes them such heart-rending and deeply frustrating experiences." [7]

A loss that occurs early in pregnancy, when the baby is identified less as an individual and more as part of the mother herself, tends to be mourned differently than a late fetal or newborn death, but grief may be very intense nevertheless. Said a diabetic woman, now in her forties, of her first unsuccessful pregnancy at age nineteen: "I remember it quite clearly. It was at thirteen weeks, so I hadn't even felt the baby move. But the pregnancy, and the child, and the *hope* were certainly a reality."

It is likely that parental investment in an unborn child begins the moment pregnancy is confirmed and builds gradually as the fetus takes on recognizably human characteristics, begins to squirm and kick, and so forth. The image of falling in love is frequently used by pregnant women to describe this feeling of a steadily deepening tie.

Not only do bereaved parents mourn the loss of the love object/fantasy child (the future doctor or lawyer, provider of grandchildren, heir to the family name) but, especially in these early casualties, the mother mourns the loss of an essential part of herself. "It feels like there's a great hole inside where the baby used to be," was the way one mother put it. Others have compared the loss to the amputation of an arm or leg, or to a sudden loss of function such as blindness or paralysis.

Pregnancy is often described as a narcissistic state, and the expectant mother's self-concept is closely tied to the well-being of her child. However ambivalent she may feel, particularly in the first months, about the prospect of parenthood, her capacity to nourish and protect this growing part of herself cannot be called into question without a massive threat to self-esteem.

One woman, who experienced multiple spontaneous abortions before her final successful pregnancy, remembers: "I come from a large Irish Catholic family, and year after year I would be the only one with no baby to diaper. My husband, who was intensely conscious of my failure to carry a pregnancy to term, used to refer to me publicly as 'the defective incubator.' Pretty soon, I began to think of myself along those lines."

In view of the importance attached by both partners to reproductive capacity, the loss of an anticipated first child is believed by many observers to be more demolishing than any subsequent pregnancy loss. However, motivations for becoming pregnant, cultural conditioning for parenthood, and the degree of maternal (or paternal) investment in a particular child vary so greatly that generalizations are always risky. In the words of Center for Preventive Psychiatry therapist Ann Kliman, "misery is not a competitive sport."

It is not even clear that a woman who has elected the traditional role of wife-mother-homemaker will be appreciably worse off following a fetal or newborn death than a career woman with varied professional interests outside the home. The latter, too, may consciously or unconsciously view motherhood as her primary role. Furthermore, since many women in dual career marriages elect to postpone motherhood until their mid-thirties or later, the medical problems involved in each pregnancy are often compounded—along with the fear that there never will be another chance.

Whatever the woman's other personal goals, a tragic outcome of pregnancy suggests a helplessness, a loss of control over her own body that comes as a terrible shock. "You think of your womb as a sheltering place, and the world as basically sheltering," commented a young woman recovering from her first unsuccessful try. "Then one day you wake up and nothing is sheltering any more."

People victimized by acute situational crises, emphasizes Ann Kliman in her book *Crisis*, "are entitled to feel whatever they feel. Responses to loss, illness, abuse, or displacement are usually neither neurotic nor psychotic; they are an *adjustment reaction* to the acute stress." [8]

It is unavoidable that a woman whose baby has died, whether before birth or after, will want to cry, talk about the event, and call forth whatever limited memories exist. Not to do this would be to deny the significance of the death, which only extends the grieving process and increases the mourner's intense preoccupation with what has been lost. Unfortunately, while the fact that the baby had little or no extrauterine life does not diminish the mother's pain, it may substantially diminish the capacity of those around her to accept that pain and support her through its resolution.

MEN, WOMEN, AND GRIEF

> He saw her from the bottom of the stairs
> Before she saw him. She was starting down,
> Looking back over her shoulder at some fear.
> She took a doubtful step and then undid it
> To raise herself and look again. He spoke
> Advancing toward her: "What is it you see
> From up there always—for I want to know."

What the woman in Robert Frost's moving "Home Burial" sees is the tiny grave of her firstborn. Her husband, well-intentioned but unable to come to grips with the acuteness of her need, confesses his frustration:

> "My words are nearly always an offense.
> I don't know how to speak of anything

So as to please you. But I might be taught
I should suppose. I can't say I see how.
A man must partly give up being a man
With women-folk. . . ."

"Give me my chance," he begs, only to lose his credibility with
her in the very next line:

"I do think, though, you overdo it a little.
What was it brought you up to think it the thing
To take your mother-loss of a first child
So inconsolably. . . ."

As their conversation dissolves into bitterness, the couple's true
emotions emerge. "It's come to this," he cries. "A man can't speak of
his own child that's dead." "You can't because you don't know how
to speak," she accuses. And later:

"You could sit there with the stains on your shoes
Of the fresh earth from your own baby's grave
And talk about your everyday concerns. . . .
I can repeat the very words you were saying.
'Three foggy mornings and one rainy day
Will rot the best birch fence a man can build.'
Think of it, talk like that at such a time!
What had how long it takes a birch to rot
To do with what was in the darkened parlor.
You *couldn't* care!" [9]

Of course, Frost's bereaved father does care, only—like many
men in our culture—he is imbued with the tight-lipped masculine
ideal and has grown out of touch with his feelings. What the poem
portrays so beautifully is not only the fact that "a man must partly
give up being a man" in order to allow neediness within himself (and
so accept it in others), but also the failure of communication that can
threaten even a basically loving partnership following a loss such as
this.

"Perhaps the clearest case for early professional intervention,"
says Dr. Mark Kaufki, a Philadelphia therapist formerly affiliated
with U.N.I.T.E. (Understanding Newborns in Traumatic Experi-

ences), "lies in the area of marital communication. Men and women react very differently to a loss of this kind and are often too bewildered, angry, and confused themselves to understand their spouse's reaction. Instead of realizing that there are a variety of legitimate ways of coping with grief, they tend to see only the differences."

Men and women do grieve differently, for a number of reasons. Although the prospective father may have a strong psychological investment in the unborn child, his knowledge of that child is strictly secondhand. The profound physiologic and emotional changes of pregnancy affect him only indirectly, and then not always in a positive fashion. Many men feel resentful and left out during their wives' pregnancies, because of the self-involvement and dreamy preoccupation which are characteristic of that state.

While the father may deeply mourn the loss of the fantasy child (the son to follow in his footsteps), he cannot share his wife's additional humiliation over the loss of *self*. Furthermore, although in the vast majority of cases neither party is actually "at fault," and despite our knowledge that certain genetic abnormalities may be transmitted via paternal, as well as maternal, inheritance, thousands of years of cultural conditioning have placed the responsibility for unsuccessful pregnancy squarely on the shoulders of the woman.

Dr. Steven P. Lindenberg, a mental health counselor in Hershey, Pennsylvania, comments: "Following the death of a child, marriages generally come under stress at two levels: the first being the woman's conviction that her husband cannot experience the depth of her grief or even empathize with it; the second being the man's suspicion that his wife's negligence, or some defect in her body, was responsible for the loss. Often these feelings are never verbalized, so that the couple finds it almost impossible to deal with them outside the therapeutic situation."

"My husband hadn't been terribly supportive during my pregnancy because he was preoccupied with problems at work," said one bereaved mother during a parents' group meeting. "Although we never really talked about it, after the miscarriage I found that very hard to forgive. In retrospect, I think I was looking for something to pin the blame on."

A man may believe that he is entirely in sympathy with his wife, yet use the excuse of unmade beds or burned toast to express anger at her for the death of their child. Or a woman may actually magnify the degree to which her husband holds her accountable for the loss—

unconsciously wishing to provoke his rejection as punishment for some imagined oversight of her own during pregnancy.

In the disillusionment that follows the realization that neither parent can fully comfort or support the other (because both are too depleted themselves), tempers flare. Ammunition is easy to come by: "I was so tired of being slow and heavy and exhausted all the time during the latter half of my pregnancy," said one mother, "that I told my husband, 'I'm sick of this; I wish the baby were dead.'" When their newborn son did die of respiratory failure shortly after birth, her husband reminded her of her words. Sometime later, he admitted that he found his reminder as hard to forgive as her initial statement: "I knew she really wanted the baby. Somehow, the words just came out. It must have made her feel terrible, but what could I do? Now, it's like there was a wall between us."

In the case of a stillbirth or neonatal death, communication is often obstructed from the moment the outcome is announced. If there has been a considerable period of hospitalization and/or care is being administered by a regional perinatal center, the father may be many miles away at the time of the baby's death. Or, if he is close at hand, he may be cautioned by a tradition-bound physician or obstetrical nurse not to allow his wife to see or touch the baby, particularly if there has been a degree of damage.

In some instances, husbands even arrange burial to coincide with the hospital recuperation period, in order to "spare" the stricken mother the experience of having to say good-bye. Many women complain of having been persuaded against their inclination to allow the hospital to take care of the upsetting details. Recalled one: "I wanted to bury the baby privately, but my husband felt very strongly that I couldn't handle that, so we signed the papers for hospital disposition. Now I have nothing—no baby and no grave to visit."

The mother has by now suffered several serious blows to her self-esteem. She has lost (1) the wished-for child, (2) decision-making power over her own body, and (3) decision-making power over the child's body. And the bereaved father is hardly better off. Having taken over primary responsibility for hospital arrangements, communications with medical staff, and telephone calls to the couple's relatives, he plunges back headlong into the world of work. Public displays of emotion are frowned upon. The destructive patterns of denial and suppression of grief become firmly established.

"It's all very well to tell men that it's okay to cry," observes

Kaufki, "but it simply isn't acceptable for a male executive to burst into tears at a conference. The same holds true for the policeman on the beat, or any other male-dominated occupation you can name. We mask our grief in order to function effectively, and then, when the time comes to interact with our partner, it's hard to switch roles."

Intent on being a tower of strength for his wife, the bereaved father may be baffled by her reluctance to be comforted. As weeks drag into months and she continues to resist his suggestions that they go out more frequently, entertain, perhaps take a vacation, his demands that she "get over it already" take on a more urgent tone. "My husband told me that he wouldn't leave for work until I cheered up a little," revealed the mother of a stillborn. "It got me so angry that I lay on the bathroom floor and pounded the tiles, screaming: 'I don't want to cheer up, damn it. *I don't feel like cheering up.*'"

In their enormously valuable book *Maternal-Infant Bonding*, Drs. Marshall H. Klaus and John H. Kennell suggest that physicians be aware of this tendency and take preventive measures when counseling bereaved couples. "The common reaction," the investigators write, "is seen of the father that he has to fight against his mourning reaction not only by keeping himself busy but also by keeping his spouse busy. It is our practice to anticipate this possibility at our first contact with the parents by saying that it is desirable to arrange to lighten up on commitments and responsibilities." [10]

Some men undertake additional jobs at this time, in part to avoid having time to brood, but also, in many instances, to meet substantial debts incurred during the hospitalization of a critically ill newborn. Few health plans cover such costs in their entirety; some cover only a small portion of the overall expense. At a time when his wife appears to be acting irrationally, the father may be reluctant to involve her in a discussion of family finances—with the result that his continued absences from home are viewed as a further rejection.

An area of special vulnerability is the couple's sexuality. Because the relationship between sexual activity and procreation can hardly be avoided, the act itself becomes a repository of painful memories. Both partners may blame themselves and one another for having initiated sexual intercourse during pregnancy, especially if this occurred following a warning from the physician to abstain or just "be careful."

There may also be arguments over when to resume sexual ac-

tivity. Medical problems may dictate that the couple avoid intercourse for several weeks, or even months, until recovery is complete.
More often, however, psychological factors are responsible for any
continuation of impaired relations between husband and wife. Depression typically produces a loss of libido, which in this case is felt
more deeply by the mother. Whereas her husband, either because he
cannot or will not allow himself to become as profoundly depressed
as she, may wish to resume relations at the earliest opportunity, the
bereaved woman may hang back, resenting the intrusion into her
space and fearful of the link between sexuality and conception. One
woman admitted, "For a long time I was afraid of having sex with my
husband. At first, he was understanding, but after a while he began to
wonder whether perhaps my feelings toward him had really changed.
Although we managed to patch things up in the end, he never really
quite got over it. He still gets angry when he thinks about it."

What a woman may perceive as callousness and insensitivity to
her needs ("All you think about is sex; don't you realize our baby is
dead?") may at least in part be based on her husband's desire to
resume emotional communication, which for some men is expressed
more easily physically than verbally. In her preoccupation with
mourning, she may ignore his signals of grief and loneliness and appear to abandon her former role as wife, mother, and helpmeet. (If
there are older children in the family, the bereaved father's caretak-
ing duties may sharply increase, adding fuel to the fire of his resentment. "It's as though she were in a cocoon. She's forgotten that the
children and I exist," is a typical comment.)

"It's so easy for problems to escalate," cautions Ann Kliman.
"The wife who submits grudgingly to her husband's demands will
evoke a response of anger and guilt. If, on the other hand, she wel-
comes his approach and is capable of arousal, she may feel guilty for
allowing herself to feel sexy under the circumstances, and unconsciously vow to be less receptive in the future."

Ultimately, this kind of physical disaffection may end the marriage and steer the bereaved mother in the direction of brief, perhaps
even homosexual, relationships. As one woman, still somewhat un-
comfortable with her new choice of lesbianism, explained: "Since my
miscarriage, I find that I cannot relate to men at all. Although I am
on good terms with my former husband, all of my subsequent relationships have been with women. I had no previous experience with

bisexuality, so I can't believe there isn't some kind of causal connection. Sex had betrayed me—and men, by implication, had betrayed me as well."

Clearly, not all marriages are subject to such severe upheaval following a tragic outcome of pregnancy. For every example of failure:

> My husband and I separated about six months after we lost the baby. We'd been having problems before, and I suppose both of us looked upon my pregnancy as a chance to save the marriage.

there are glowing examples of success:

> I don't know if there are words sufficient to describe what it meant for us to have gone through this together. We found a degree of closeness that we hadn't even known existed in our relationship.

But the demands placed on both partners are so overwhelming that the possibility of a breakup is dramatically increased—thus, the advisability of seeking professional guidance *before* communication has ground completely to a halt.

In *The Bereaved Parent*, Harriet Sarnoff Schiff writes: "Our culture has given us to understand that when a couple marry, two people are joined and become one. In many aspects this may well be true, but that ideal often shatters with the death of a child. Suddenly, and frighteningly, this couple, this two wedded into one, has a basic truth thrust upon it. Once again they are two. . . . The couple, unlike when they laughed together, vacationed together, shared downfalls together, suddenly finds at the time of the greatest tragedy in their lives—and at the time of their greatest need—that each is an individual. They must mourn as individuals. Separately." [11]

The strength of the relationship prior to bereavement, and what each partner is able to bring into the situation in the form of earlier experiences in dealing with frustration and defeat, heavily influence the denouement. However, these are not the only factors. Inadequate community recognition of the loss and insensitive handling of parental needs by caregivers during the period of hospitalization may be equally significant determinants of the outcome of mourning.

In the following chapters, we will examine the effect of society's response to fetal and newborn death and explore what has been and is currently being done by parent support groups, hospital personnel, and clergy to promote healthy expression of grief and reduce the threat to family integrity.

2
The Community's Response

A CENTURY AGO in rural America, to lose an infant in childbed meant to be deluged with callers and unsolicited advice from grandmothers, aunts, and neighbors who, in all statistical likelihood, would have each lost several children themselves. Of course, much of the advice was faulty, because scientific understanding of the causes and consequences of reproductive casualty was far less advanced than today. But there was an openness in the community response to death, a lack of evasiveness which made it easier for parents to mourn—and ultimately get back to the business of living.

Even as recently as fifty years ago, birth and death were highly visible events. Reminiscing about his childhood in northern Maine, pediatrician Raymond Duff of Yale-New Haven Hospital recalls: "I grew up at a time and in a place where tuberculosis, diarrhea, measles, and rheumatic fever were everyday killers. We dug the graves ourselves, and we carried our dead to those graves. So as a small boy, I already had an instinctive understanding of the terms of living. You played in the soil as a child, you worked it as an adult, and finally you died and went back to it."

No sane person would suggest a return to the days of higher perinatal mortality. But it is valuable to remember, when we speak of heroic efforts to improve the prognosis for high-risk newborns, that one of the less positive consequences of our increasing reliance on regional intensive care has been to cut community awareness of obstetrical losses to a minimum.

Community support, however, is lacking only in part because death is less public today. A number of factors work in concert to isolate bereaved parents and discourage outsiders from making contact, among them: (1) the breakdown and geographical scattering of the extended family; (2) our mobile society, which encourages formation of casual friendships rather than the deep and lasting ties that evolved when neighbors lived alongside one another for generations; and (3) the anonymity and suspicion that have come to characterize life in our large urban centers. "No man is an island," wrote John Donne early in the seventeenth century. He would find it more difficult to find support for his views today.

BACKGROUND: GRIEF AS SOCIAL STIGMA

Talk to me about the truth of religion and I'll listen gladly. Talk to me about the duty of religion and I'll listen submissively. But don't come talking to me about the consolations of religion or I shall suspect that you don't understand.

Unless, of course, you can literally believe all that stuff about family reunions 'on the further shore,' pictured in entirely earthly terms. But that is all unscriptural, all out of bad hymns and lithographs. There's not a word of it in the Bible. And it rings false.

—C. S. Lewis,
A GRIEF OBSERVED

Without a firm foothold in the community, we are much more vulnerable when disaster strikes. Psychologist Louise J. Kaplan observes that: "Our disenchantments with funeral arrangements and cemetery rituals, our inability to share our sorrows, our shame at admitting temporary helplessness and hopelessness, our cynicism toward any public display of caring or concern, our hurried, crowded lives that have no time or room for the unwelcome anxieties and letdowns that are essential aspects of our humanness—all these force us to lock up grief, to confront our personal crises as though we were all alone in the world, as though there were no one to turn to." [1]

Although a minority continue to seek refuge in the consolations of religion, many young families find the elaborate rituals that comforted their ancestors neither comforting nor meaningful. And with dwindling church and synagogue attendance has come a parallel decline in the social value of religion: the uniting of family and community.

Sociologist Robert Fulton notes that the current trend toward immediate disposition of the dead and stiff-upper-lipped repression of normal grief "is in sharp contrast with our social past as well as with our present knowledge regarding the dynamics of personal, irreparable loss." [2] A funeral, says Fulton, has purpose not only in disposing of the remains and publicly acknowledging the significance of the event, but also in asserting the continuity of the group as a whole. However, he too admits that "a ceremony that no longer appropriately symbolizes the understood meaning of a death, or fails correctly to dramatize the change that has overtaken the living and the dead, can create only confusion, if not anger and frustration, on the part of the bereaved." [3]

The problem goes beyond the fact that the traditional rituals often appear simplistic and alien to our scientifically sophisticated eyes. Their underlying foundation, belief in an afterlife in which the just will be rewarded and earthly suffering remedied, has been severely shaken. "Suffering," says Dr. Elisabeth Kübler-Ross, "has lost its meaning." Paradoxically, even if we continue to take advantage of the church's socializing function, without intrinsic faith "we are deprived of the church's former purpose, namely, to give hope, a purpose in tragedies here on earth, and an attempt to understand and bring meaning to otherwise inacceptable painful occurrences in our life." [4]

In the mid-1960s, Geoffrey Gorer, a British anthropologist, made a comprehensive study of mourning practices in his native land and found that abandonment of many of the social and religious rituals had resulted in a nationwide increase of maladaptive responses to the loss of a loved person. "At present," Gorer observes, "death and mourning are treated with much the same prudery as sexual impulses were a century ago. Then it was held, quite sincerely, that good women, or ladies, had no sexual impulses, and that good men, or gentlemen, could keep theirs under complete control by strength of will or character. Today it would seem to be believed, quite sincerely, that sensible, rational men and women can keep their mourning under complete control by strength of will or character so that it need be given no public expression, and indulged, if at all, in private, as furtively as if it were an analogue of masturbation." [5]

Giving way to grief today is viewed as being morbid, unhealthy, and demoralizing for those around the bereaved as well as for the mourner himself. Friends and acquaintances urge participation in outside activities and beg the survivor not to "dwell on it so much." As a result, many of those interviewed by Gorer had chosen to lock up their grief and suffer in private, while others simply denied their feelings, even to themselves. Unfortunately, says Gorer, denial of one's own grief has a way of leading to denial of grief in others (see "Men, Women, and Grief," p. 28), which can result in a general attitude of indifference toward the public good.

What we are faced with today, says Gorer, is a "pornography of death" in which the natural processes of corruption and decay have become too disgusting for public acknowledgment. Our dead are unrealistically beautified; our children told that they are merely asleep or awaiting reincarnation in the form of grass, trees, and flowers. As sex was to our Victorian forebears, death has become the twentieth-century taboo.

American social scientist Ernest Becker goes one step further. Citing a number of contemporary theoreticians, Becker challenges Freud's hypothesis that human culture is based upon repression because man is first and foremost a seeker of sexual gratification. Human culture *is* based upon repression, Becker argues, not because man is primarily a seeker of pleasure but because he is primarily an avoider of death. Although the sexual urge is powerful, it is subordinate to a greater "curse"—consciousness of death, and the repression of that consciousness. "The idea of death, the fear of it," Becker writes, "haunts the human animal like nothing else; it is a mainspring of human activity—activity designed largely to avoid the fatality of death, to overcome it by denying in some way that it is the final destiny for man." [6]

Deprived of the sense of spiritual community embodied in thousands of years of Judeo-Christian teaching, we are brought face to face with our own existential anxieties concerning death. Rather than reach some acceptable *modus vivendi*, we retreat by denying that the event has any relevance to us at all. We rely on science to defeat human frailty and avoid any reference to the subject or contact with the bereaved—who, in the framework of competition with death, are clearly the "losers."

A SPECIAL LOSS

They greeted me with great enthusiasm, as though I'd been
sick with a foot or ear ailment and was now beginning to
convalesce. They congratulated me for carrying my work
through to the end despite-the-difficulties. They took me
out to eat. And never a word about you. When I tried to
say something, they assumed an expression between evasiveness and embarrassment: almost as though I were bringing
up a disagreeable subject and they wanted to say let's-not-
think-about-it-any-more-what-has-been-has-been.
                              —*Oriana Fallaci*,
                              Letter to a Child Never Born

While denial is a common element in the public reaction to all
forms of bereavement, parents who have experienced a fetal or newborn death are often hardest hit. Because there may be little objec-
tive evidence of their baby's existence, the episode is easily dismissed
from the minds of relatives, friends, and co-workers as something to
be gotten over as quickly as possible. "Everybody thinks in terms of
a timetable," complained one exhausted mother whose third pregnancy terminated abruptly in the twenty-fourth week. "If the baby
died in the sixth month, you're not supposed to feel as much grief as
if he'd died at term. After a while, you stop arguing and just let them
talk."

If loss was due to a spontaneous abortion, few of the couple's
acquaintances may even have known about the pregnancy. The
mother may return to work and/or normal household routines within
a week of discharge and hesitate to burden colleagues or neighbors
with her grief.

Even in the case of stillbirth, there is rarely a formal funeral
service or a gravesite to visit. Often the baby is not even named
(although very few couples ever use a once-chosen first name for a
subsequent child). If a decision is made in favor of hospital removal
of the body, parents often receive little or no information about the
location and circumstances of interment.

The lack of concrete facts concerning the events of birth and
death has been compared to the situation of a family whose husband
or son is reported "missing in action" in wartime. Whereas in the case

of a soldier reported "killed" there is at least a body to mourn, these families continue their psychological search for the missing party long after all realistic hope has been extinguished.*

"Memory," says Emanuel Lewis, "facilitates mourning." With a spontaneous abortion, stillbirth, or neonatal death there may be very little to remember, particularly if the mother was heavily anesthetized during delivery and/or sedated afterward. Well-meaning friends and relatives often remove the crib and baby clothes so that the mother will not be troubled by them on her return from the hospital. One woman who had miscarried in mid-pregnancy found the magazine section of her local newspaper unexpectedly missing; her mother had hidden it because the cover story dealt with newborns. "I knew her intention was to protect me," she said, "but I resented the fact that my mother wanted me to pretend it didn't happen. It did happen, and I wanted to cry and talk about it."

A woman who seeks out her friends for consolation may be surprised to find many of them becoming awkward and silent not only on the subject of her loss, but on any topic related to childbirth or parenting. One bereaved mother, whose friends had adamantly refused to let her discuss the appearance of her stillborn son and her reactions to the death, found herself writing long, descriptive letters to old acquaintances, just so that she could see the baby's name in print.

"I needed to talk about Jonathan," she explained. "He was my baby and like any mother, I was proud. I wanted to tell my friends what he looked like, that his hair had been brown and his eyes blue. But nobody asked. Everyone expected that, because he hadn't lived, I would want to forget the details. But the details were important; they were my lifeline."

Details *are* important. Talking or writing about the event helps to retrieve repressed memories, aiding in the work of mourning. Many women find that keeping a diary, even if it consists of nothing

---

* Searching is a normal and characteristic feature of bereavement. Rather than avoiding locations in which the dead might otherwise be found, the mourner purposely seeks them out. Although on a conscious level she realizes that such hopes are irrational, a mother may follow carriages in the park or peer into another shopper's cart at the supermarket, looking for her dead baby. The activity of searching, especially in the early months of bereavement, may be all-consuming and leave little room for such customary interests as food, sleep, personal appearance, work, or family. Gradually, as the months pass, the mourner begins to accept that the dead will not return, and interest in the outside world resumes.

more than jottings in a spiral notebook, gives them a sense of peace, as though by committing the event to paper they were securing its place in history. "Even with a live birth," says Emanuel Lewis, "the mother feels a sense of loss, but the consolation of a surviving 'outside baby' helps the mother overcome her bewildering sadness at losing her 'inside baby.' With a stillbirth [or any fetal loss], however, there is an outer as well as an inner void." [7]

Widening the gap between the bereaved mother and her associates is the outsiders' inability to grasp the magnitude of her pain. "You have to defend your right to grieve," said one angry woman some months after her third child was stillborn, "as though the baby hadn't really been a person and you hadn't really been its mother." "All of my friends were shocked and frightened when I miscarried," said another. "But they handled it very differently. Some simply withdrew. Others were able to deal with their discomfort, as long as I was the one who introduced the subject. Finally, there was a third group of friends who encouraged me to talk, who would bring up the experience without waiting to be asked. Those were the ones who really helped."

"You find out who your friends are," is a very common response among women who have experienced a fetal or newborn death. Unfortunately, even the best-intentioned people often have no idea of what is expected of them, and blunders are frequent. "I was angry at my sister," one mother recalled, "because she had waited for me to call and tell her about it, rather than making the first move. She told me afterward that she had been afraid of rejection. I felt that in her place, I would have risked rejection, and I told her so."

Harriet Sarnoff Schiff suggests that, unfair or not, responsibility for making the first contact with a friend or relative usually rests with the bereaved parent. The degree of unease with which society regards the mourner is such that a potential helper can find innumerable excuses for not calling, writing, or dropping by in person after a loss. With the passage of time, guilt is added to the burden of not knowing what to say. Ultimately, the whole issue becomes so embarrassing that the caller decides to forgo the friendship, rather than broach the subject with the bereaved.

"As a rule, people seemed much more comfortable sending gifts than actually sitting down with me and talking about what happened," one woman said. "I remember thinking, as I unwrapped one of the gifts: Why are they doing this? It isn't my birthday!"

Even if a friend or relative does summon up the courage to call, the result is often disastrous. Trivial conversations, begun in order not to upset the family, are rejected for the distracting ploys that they are. Homilies such as "It's for the best" or "It was God's will" rarely provide comfort and are more often seen as threatening in their implications. ("What kind of a God is it that destroys little children?" is a typical response.)

Similarly, the suggestion that the couple "can have another baby" is counterproductive, in that it negates both the individuality of the dead child and the parents' right to mourn for him or her. True, in most instances a couple who have experienced an early fetal or perinatal death can proceed to have one or many more healthy children; but these are not, nor should they be considered, replacements for the one who died.

The speaker in William Kotzwinkle's *Swimmer in the Secret Sea* is the couple's obstetrician, but his comment—and the young father's perception of it—are classic:

> "The baby looks perfectly normal," said Barker. "There's no reason why you can't have another child."
> Laski listened numbly. He thinks that's what has been at stake, our wish for a child, any child, not this particular child who swung down the road between us. They can't know how special he is. They point to the future. But we're here, forever, now.[8]

If there already are older siblings in the family, the reminder that the couple "ought to be thankful" for their existence is equally resented. In all likelihood, the parents *are* thankful; however, that doesn't diminish their sense of failure and injustice this time around. A preschooler or school-aged child is already to a large extent an independently functioning individual. Packing a lunchbox or supervising homework may be satisfying activities, but they do not compensate for the loss of a tiny, helpless infant or for the emptiness a mother feels. "You have a physical need to hold something," said one. "Whenever I heard a baby cry, my arms literally ached. To fill that gap, I would walk around the house with a pillow clutched to my chest. I'm sure my husband thought that I was going crazy."

Another frequently heard comment is: "I know how you feel." Chances are good that, unless the visitor is another bereaved parent, he or she does not know. Investigators of the mourning process concur that the death of a sibling or a parent, however painful, is different in *quality* from the death of a child.*

Pastoral counselor Sherron Hughes-Tremper has drawn up a set of suggestions for helping bereaved parents deal with the bumbling responses of friends and family. First, says Hughes-Tremper, "you will have to decide how much you will let pass or will disagree . . . a clear and direct statement of your own feelings works better than an argument or attack." As examples of such clear and direct statements, she offers:

- No, I don't agree with that.
- I feel this way about it.
- I don't think of my baby's death in that way.
- What you are saying doesn't comfort me.
- I know you are well-meaning, but . . .
- A lot of people believe that, but I don't find it comforting.
- I still feel angry, but can't discuss it.[9]

It helps to be assertive enough to let callers know, calmly but firmly, when an intrusion is unwelcome. This mother felt afterward that she had handled her grief very well: "I knew what I needed and made certain that I got it. If a friend called at a time when I didn't feel like talking, I just said so and hung up as politely as I could. Or, if I sensed that someone was trying to take my mind off what happened by talking about politics or the weather, I would say, 'Look, I want to talk about my baby. If you can accept that, fine. If not, we'll just have to finish this conversation another time.' "

Unfortunately, to a couple struggling through the "angry" phase of bereavement, just about any comment may sound wrong, for in fact no words of condolence can really achieve the desired effect (i.e., making up for the loss itself). Colin Murray Parkes notes that "pain is inevitable in such a case and cannot be avoided. It stems from the awareness of both parties that neither can give the other what he wants. The helper cannot bring back the person who is dead and the bereaved person cannot gratify the helper by seeming helped. No

---

* The death of an older child, toward whom deep affectional bonds have already developed, is undoubtedly the greatest tragedy of all. Even in these early losses, however, there is a sense of futility and unnaturalness which is seen less frequently following the death of an aging parent or grown sibling. Although we may dread it, we anticipate that our parents will die. We take for granted, on the other hand, that our children will outlive us.

wonder that both feel dissatisfied with the encounter."[10]

And yet, Parkes adds, the bereaved do appreciate sincere expressions of sympathy paid to them by others. While there is no formula for finding the right thing to say, he suggests that an obvious willingness to sit and listen quietly to the mourner's story is appreciated more than speechmaking.

"Family and friends called and wrote—from miles away," one woman recalled. "They didn't try to give advice or offer platitudes. One friend just wrote 'I cry for you' on a small card. The outpouring of kindness was amazing; I told people I could feel their caring wrapped all around us, like a blanket."

The most meaningful gestures are frequently the purely spontaneous ones. One author tells of a condolence call made in a bathing suit—the caller simply arrived at the family's door as soon as she heard the news. Or the assistance may be of a very practical nature, as this couple found out after their first child was stillborn: "We live in a friendly neighborhood, and the people next door—they're the most wonderful neighbors one could ask for. Before we left for the hospital, we told them that I felt no movement and it looked as though the baby might be dead. We came home some days later to find our walk shoveled; they had also picked up our mail and left a huge jar of homemade vegetable soup for us."

It is sad that so few parents who experience a fetal or newborn death have the benefit of neighbors such as the couple described above. Too often, the community response is predictable by its *absence*, as this mother learned under similar circumstances: "I found that telling people [about the stillbirth] was terribly hard. After a while, I began to expect the dead silence on the telephone, or that horrified look in someone's eyes that tells you, 'Don't go any further.'"

Gorer notes that the majority of human societies have developed formal rituals for assisting mourners through what amounts to a rite of passage—from the period immediately following the death, through a stage of relative seclusion and withdrawal from society, and finally into a gradual return to normal social functioning. During this period there are communal ceremonies focusing on the event of death, and the bereaved are distinguished from other members of the society (whether tribal Indian or nineteenth-century British middle class) by peculiarities of appearance, dress, or social mannerism. "If a custom, such as this, is very widespread throughout human societies at all stages of development," the anthropologist concludes, "it seems reasonable to assume that the custom is congruent with species-characteristic human psychology; and, as a corollary, those aberrant societies which lack such a custom are failing to provide their members with the support which most societies make available." [11]

THE ROLE OF PARENT SUPPORT GROUPS IN FACILITATING MOURNING

As a solution to what he perceives as the isolation of the mourner in contemporary society, Gorer proposes institution of rites of "civil mourning" analogous to our present rite of civil marriage. Such secular rituals would take into account (1) the need of the mourner for both privacy and companionship, (2) the desirability of expressing grief without social embarrassment, and (3) the likelihood that mourning will be accompanied by signs of somatic distress, such as fatigue, insomnia, and loss of appetite.

It is a positive sign that, while fifteen years ago such "socially acceptable" opportunities for grief work may have existed only in the author's mind, today this is no longer the case. In both Britain and the United States, independent parent support groups such as The Society of Compassionate Friends, A.M.E.N.D. (Aiding A Mother Experiencing Neonatal Death), and P.E.P.D. (Parents Experiencing Perinatal Death), and hospital-affiliated bereavement clinics such as the Perinatal Bereavement Clinic at State University of New York Downstate Medical Center, provide bereaved parents with a sympathetic forum for discussing their memories of the past, immediate emotional needs, and hopes and fears for the future.

Some grief process groups are composed predominantly of couples who have experienced a death during the course of pregnancy. Others are open to anyone who has either experienced perinatal death or given birth to a living mentally or physically handicapped child. Certain parent organizations, such as The Society of Compassionate Friends, encourage attendance by all bereaved parents regardless of the age of the child at the time of death. There are also groups to deal with specific problems, such as parental infertility (e.g., RESOLVE).

Meetings are generally monthly or biweekly. The discussion may be led by a psychologist or social worker, or discussion may take place informally, without benefit of professional leadership. Some organizations of bereaved parents do not hold regular meetings at all, but sponsor workshops in hospitals, nursing schools, and religious institutions and refer newly bereaved couples to trained "listeners" who have direct knowledge of the experience, having gone through it themselves.

Although designed to meet the urgent need of bereaved parents for information and support, most groups also welcome the participation of concerned relatives, friends, and health-care workers. Almost all are nonsectarian. As stated in the literature supplied by The Society of Compassionate Friends, "Grief and sorrow are subject to no geographical, ethnic, or credal barriers."

A couple may be referred to a local group by their hospital chaplain or social worker, by a member of the obstetrical team, or by their pediatrician. Often parents will wait a few weeks or months before joining, on the assumption that hearing about the tragedies of others will cause them to become even more depressed. Dr. Marion Cohen, a mathematician, poet, and bereaved mother, recalls having a somewhat different response: "I remember envisioning the group as being something like the local PTA. A bunch of typical organization-type supermothers. After all," reasoned Cohen, ". . . I've never before fit in with a group of people just picked at random. Why should *this* be any exception?" [12]

Another deterrent for some parents is the stigma attached to any type of psychotherapeutic assistance. Already plagued by guilt and frightened by the emotional intensity of their responses, either or both partners may feel defensive about joining an organization predicated on the idea that *the bereaved do need help.* Some couples only look into the services offered by a group several years—and a number of healthy children—after a loss.

Having taken the step, however, most parents are relieved and enthusiastic. "I found myself looking forward to the next meeting with an urgency bordering on hunger," says Cohen. "For the first time since it happened, I was actually looking forward to something."[13]

For many mothers, joining a group-support organization represents the first step in a long and painful process of readjustment. The pressure-free atmosphere of the group and the knowledge that she can either talk or remain silent, cry or laugh, without anyone thinking her behavior bizarre or becoming bored by the repetitiveness of her story, may give a mother the incentive to really unburden herself for the first time: "The wonderful thing about a parents' group is that you don't have to feel guilty talking about your experience. Other friends may be willing to listen, but there's a line beyond which you become a burden. In the group situation, nobody's a burden because everyone understands that by talking, you are not only helping yourself but also the others in the group."

Over and over again, parents remark about the accepting atmosphere of group meetings and the value of comparing notes or simply exchanging words of comfort with people who really understand. "It's very hard for those who haven't gone through the experience to just sit and listen, knowing that there is nothing they can do to help you," explained one mother already pregnant with another child. "And yet, when people shut you out through their own inability to cope with bereavement, in effect what they are saying is that you have no right to your feelings. What is needed are listeners who can accept your feelings simply because they are an honest expression of *you*."

"We don't compare our griefs," observes Cohen, "we don't make it into a contest. Sure, those who lost two babies suffered more than twice as much as those who lost only one, but that doesn't negate the single tragedy." [14]

In the process of going over memories of the hospital experience, new aspects of the pregnancy and/or birth often come to light. Others may prompt a bereaved couple for specific details (weight, length, hair and eye color), knowing that such information will help the parents form a clearer mental picture of the child-that-was.* Practical questions are also discussed: Where to go for genetic testing? What types of burial are available? Should the baby be named? Will a birth and death certificate have to be filed?

As valuable as the meetings themselves is the support network that is created. Couples understand and share with one another the anticipation and trepidations of later pregnancies. Group members who have gone through the initial crisis may return (often with babies in tow) to share their expertise with couples only recently bereaved. Although attendance by both partners is ideal, a bereaved mother

---

* Without such a mental picture, grieving is very difficult. As mentioned earlier, one of the handicaps parents face in mourning a loss such as this is the tendency of society to view the fetus as a nonperson, and the death as a nonevent.

attending by herself can gain new insight into the marital conflicts that often accompany grief, which in turn may generate more frank and effective dialogues with her husband. If a mother does not feel up to the challenge of open discussion, a member may call at her home for a private "rap."

In a social system hardly noted for responsiveness to its needy, the self-help group offers a constructive and flexible format for assisting families through the rite of passage of bereavement and back into the larger community.

For a state-by-state listing of established support groups and examples of specific services such groups can provide, see Appendix.

3
Mothers' Voices: The Work of Mourning

Whaddaya mean, *Mother* Nature? Nature's no mother.

If Nature were a mother, women would ovulate once a day, not once a month. And umbilical cords would be rigid pipes instead of flexible ropes that can twist and turn and do God-knows-what to the baby. And placentas wouldn't have all those veins and be so complicated. And it would be impossible for embryos to implant anywhere but the uterus, and all babies that were meant to be miscarriages wouldn't implant in the first place. And women wouldn't have morning sickness when their babies were doing just fine and feel top o' the morning when their babies were suffocating.

And if Nature were a mother, it wouldn't be "survival of the fittest." It would be "survival of the sweetest."

So Whaddaya mean, Mother Nature? Nature's no mother. If Nature were a mother, there would be no "accidents of Nature." If Nature were a mother, Nature would be perfect.

THE ANGRY VOICE above belongs to Marion Cohen, whose third child, Kerin, died at age forty-four hours. Like so many of the women quoted in this book, Cohen's response to perinatal death was to feverishly take up her pad and pencil.

"I don't know how I would have made it through the situation without being able to verbalize it in some way," she says. "You don't have to be a writer. Anyone can keep a diary. The important thing is to put down your thoughts, because there are so many small things that can be forgotten and so many emotional changes. I found the greatest relief in poetry—the discipline of the rhythms clarified my thinking."

What do women who have been through a reproductive casualty write about? The intensity of their emotional responses, for one thing . . . what they have learned about themselves and their husbands or lovers . . . their relationship to God, to their friends, to their mothers . . . the terrible loneliness of bereavement . . . and, months and even years after the loss, the lingering memories.

> I have two wombs now.
> One of them is outside my body.
> It moves around; it changes size; it changes shape.
> Sometimes it looks like a coffin; sometimes it
>   looks like a cloud; sometimes it looks like a
>   regular womb, bobbing behind like a colostomy.
> Its rules are different.
> E.g., It is always pregnant.
> Sometimes it goes into labor.
> Sometimes the labor is short, sometimes long.
> Sometimes the birth is moving, sometimes still.
> A double uterus now.
> Cord connecting the two.
>
> In my Cesarean days, this womb bears down.
> In my hysterectomy days, this womb will float on.
> (In my grandmother days, I will have my own baby.)
> In my dead days, this womb will continue,
> Growing, contracting, bearing down, bleeding, for-
>   ever after, I will never forget it.
>   —*Marion Cohen,*
>   "KERIN POEM, TWO YEARS LATER"

Although this chapter begins with an overview of the scientific literature, the real heart of what it means to be a bereaved mother is contained in the words of the mothers themselves:

"I was shocked by how alone I felt. You grow up thinking that your family and friends will stand behind you, you get married thinking that your husband will stand behind you, and to a certain degree they all did. But in the last analysis, I felt that it was *my* tragedy, my pain. . . . My husband was wonderful. He took days off from work, he shopped, he cooked. Others helped out, too. Still, it wasn't enough. It seemed as though *nothing would ever be enough*."

AFTERSHOCKS

In what, now, does the work which mourning performs consist? I do not think there is anything far-fetched in presenting it in the following way. Reality-testing has shown that the loved object no longer exists, and it proceeds to demand that all libido shall be withdrawn from its attachments to that object. This demand arouses understandable opposition. . . . Normally, respect for reality gains the day. Nevertheless its orders cannot be obeyed at once. They are carried out bit by bit, at great expense of time and cathectic energy. . . .

—*Sigmund Freud,*
MOURNING AND MELANCHOLIA

Stages of Grief

The recent popular interest in thanatology has by now familiarized American readers with many of the characteristics of the human encounter with death (or other great loss). To recap the conclusions of Dr. Elisabeth Kübler-Ross and others, grief typically follows a progressive course consisting of five rather distinct stages: denial and isolation, anger, bargaining, depression, and acceptance of the loss.

These may vary considerably depending upon the individual's ability to prepare for the loss, extent of isolation or family support, existence of strong religious convictions, and so on. Two or more stages may also coexist, so that painful facts which are perceived clearly one minute may be suppressed the next. Or, just when the mourner is convinced that he or she is ready to face the future with equanimity, an "anniversary" may provide the occasion for a new outburst of despair.

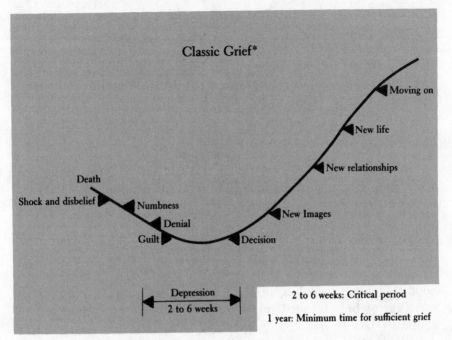

Classic Grief*

Death

Shock and disbelief

Numbness

Denial

Guilt

Decision

New Images

New relationships

New life

Moving on

Depression
2 to 6 weeks

2 to 6 weeks: Critical period

1 year: Minimum time for sufficient grief

Reprinted from *Perinatology-Neonatology*, Nov./Dec. 1977, p. 31. Copyright by Barrington Publications, Inc., 825 S. Barrington Ave., Los Angeles, California 90049.

As C. S. Lewis commented, sometime after the death of his wife, "Grief is like a long valley, a winding valley where any bend may reveal a totally new landscape. . . . Sometimes the surprise is the opposite one; you are presented with exactly the same sort of country you thought you had left behind miles ago. That is when you wonder whether the valley isn't a circular trench. But it isn't. There are partial recurrences, but the sequence doesn't repeat." [1]

The five-stage model, then, is exactly that—a model. However, it is valuable on several counts: first, for the insight it gives into the universality of grieving as a response to loss; second, as an indication that there can be multiple variations upon a single theme (say, anger) without departing from the theme itself; and third, as a general index of how particular individuals are progressing in their attempt to accept the loss, place it in the context of other life experiences, and start to make positive plans for the future.

Psychiatrist-author Gilbert Kliman divides the work of mourning into three general areas: testing and accepting the reality of the loss; remembering—working over and reducing emotional investment in memories concerning the lost object; and cultivating new object relationships.

Elements of both of these outlines may be seen in the following trajectory of classic grief, drawn up by James D. Thullen, D.O., of the Department of Pediatrics, University of North Carolina School of Medicine, Chapel Hill.

Symptoms of Grief

In what is considered the classic study of the symptomatology of acute grief, Erich Lindemann, M.D., of Harvard Medical School interviewed 101 bereaved disaster victims (survivors of the Coconut Grove fire in Boston) and other persons who had lost close relatives as a result of war or terminal illness. The picture they presented, Lindemann reported, was remarkably uniform, including: "sensations of somatic distress occurring in waves lasting from twenty minutes to an hour at a time, a feeling of tightness in the throat, choking with shortness of breath, need for sighing, and an empty feeling in the abdomen, lack of muscular power, and an intense subjective distress described as tension or mental pain." [2]

Survivors complained of digestive symptoms ("The food tastes like sand." "I have no appetite at all."), feelings of increased emotional distance from other people, and preoccupation with images of the deceased.* There was a marked tendency to search the past for evidence that the survivor had not done right by the dead, and feelings of guilt were nearly universal. There was also a tendency to respond with irritability and anger to the overtures of friends and relatives—which conflicted sharply with the needs of the bereaved for assistance and actually frightened many of those interviewed, who mistook their own hostility for evidence of mental illness.

Lindemann observed that, contrary to the survivors' claims of exhaustion ("Everything I lift seems so heavy. The slightest effort makes me feel exhausted."), the majority of mourners displayed a compulsive restlessness and inability to sit still. Activities were not pursued in an organized, productive fashion, however. Rather, there was a continuous search for something to do, which generally ended in frustration. "Nothing seems to promise reward," the psychiatrist

---

* In the case of women bereaved by a fetal or newborn death, this is seen in the mother's intense desire to form a mental picture of the infant as a prelude to mourning.

writes, "only the ordinary activities of the day are carried on, and these in a routine manner, falling apart into small steps, each of which has to be carried out with much effort and without zest." [3]

The duration of symptoms, he concluded, appeared to depend upon the success with which the mourner pursued so-called "*grief work,* namely, emancipation from the bondage to the deceased, re-adjustment to the environment in which the deceased is missing, and the formation of new relationships." [4] When grieving was delayed or appeared to be blocked completely, later "morbid" or distorted reactions—including the development of recognized medical conditions such as ulcerative colitis, rheumatoid arthritis, and asthma—were observed.

(Psychiatric management then consisted of helping the mourner uncover and work through his grief responses and restructure his relationship with the deceased. When this was accomplished, satisfying patterns of social interaction could once again be found.)

Colin Murray Parkes describes three attributes as dominating grief work:

- Preoccupation with thoughts of the lost person, which Parkes suggests derives from the urge to search for that person. (The mourner's endless quest for something to do derives from the same source.)
- Painful, repetitive recollection of the loss experience, which is the equivalent of worry work and results in acceptance of the loss as irrevocable.
- An attempt to make sense of the loss, to fit it into the mourner's larger world picture.

"The most characteristic feature of grief," Parkes writes, "is not prolonged depression but acute and episodic 'pangs.' A pang of grief is an episode of severe anxiety and pychological pain. At such a time the lost person is strongly missed and the survivor sobs or cries aloud for him.

"Pangs of grief begin within a few hours or days of bereavement and usually reach a peak of severity within five to fourteen days. At first they are very frequent and seem to occur spontaneously but as time passes they become less frequent and take place only when something occurs that brings the loss to mind." [5]

One mother compared the sensation to having "a clock inside my body that worked without my knowing it was there. On the anniversary of the [stillborn] baby's death I would become terribly blue, and so possessive that I wouldn't let the new baby out of my sight. The next day, I'd check the calendar and, sure enough, another month had rolled around. . . ."

Especially difficult days for bereaved parents include Mother's Day, Father's Day, Christmas, and the baby's due date or birth date. The arrival of infant-care magazines or advertisements for baby products, television programs describing methods of childbirth or featuring topics of interest to new parents, or simply the sight of another mother wheeling a carriage or stroller may also provoke an attack of pining for what was lost.

Listening to women recreate their hospital experiences in detail, even years afterward; hearing them describe significant alterations in their relationships with husbands, parents, co-workers, older children; observing them grapple with anger and despair and, later, the innumerable short episodes in which memory comes flooding back, we are again struck by the fact that this is a crisis with continuing repercussions. Like an underground ripple in the wake of some massive earthquake, the shock waves generated by a fetal or newborn death stretch far into the future, affecting every aspect of the woman's life from that day forward.

A SLOW EVOLUTION

Don't look at me that way
Just ask Is this your first?
Don't look at me that way
Just ask me What's her name?
Don't look at me that way
It isn't over yet.
Don't look at me that way
Just play along with me.
—*Marion Cohen,*
"Intensive Care Nursery, II"

Denial and Isolation

"Not me." "This isn't really happening." "It's all a bad dream— any moment now I'll wake up." Typically, the announcement that an unborn or newborn child is in critical danger is greeted with frozen disbelief.

When death is confirmed, shock is redoubled. The mother may challenge the obstetrician to try the fetal heart once again. Often, especially if the outcome was unexpected, the parents are too numb even to cry. "Both tears and the absence of tears are perfectly normal," observes pediatrician Raymond Duff of Yale-New Haven Hospital. "People have all sorts of ways of adapting to catastrophe. Temporary hysterical laughter is not unusual, either; Shakespeare introduced comic relief into his tragedies for a reason."

The first day passes in a fog. Instructions regarding the completion of legal forms and medical explanations of the cause of death are barely understood. If she is ambulatory, the mother may drift down to the nursery, hoping to discover that a miracle has occurred or the staff have lied, and her baby is really there.

There is a sense, also, of being cut off from the life of the hospital and even from the consoling words of visitors. The mother's own voice—asking questions of doctors and nurses, relaying the news to relatives, comforting her other children via telephone—may sound to her as though it were coming from far away, from a body not her own.

> Mercifully,
> Unreality takes over.
> It happened and it happened, but not to me. . . .
> —*Marion Cohen,*
> FROM "DOES TIME HEAL ALL WOUNDS?"

Denial and isolation serve a valuable function. Rather than allow itself to become overwhelmed by the immensity of the loss, the victim's mind anesthetizes itself—permitting her to assimilate the information in gradual stages. "The theory of psychic defense," explains Parkes, "rests on the assumption that there is a limit to the amount of anxiety an individual can tolerate and that when this limit is reached the individual will defend himself by withdrawing, psychologically, from the situation that evokes the anxiety." [6]

Opposing this defensive retreat is the mind's reality-testing tendency, which demands that the experience be recollected in minute detail before it can be accepted as fact. These conflicting tendencies alternate throughout the mourning process—the former dominating the first phase, the latter slowly gaining prominence with the passage of time. Thus, a mother may allow herself to weep over her baby's blanket or photograph one moment and shield herself from a similarly direct confrontation the next. Protective devices may be conscious, as in the bereaved parent's determination, often encouraged by relatives and medical staff, to "think about other things." Or they may be unconscious, as in her early refusal to accept the physician's verdict of death or, much later, in the overwhelming lassitude which makes even performance of routine household tasks a challenge.

Remembering that she had "wandered around in a daze" for a month or more following her baby's stillbirth, one woman recalled: "I'd stop in the middle of sentences, forgetting what I'd meant to say. I lost things. I bumped into things. What finally brought me to my senses was a near-disaster. I'd left a pot of soup simmering on the stove and gone upstairs to take yet another nap. . . . The smell of burning brought me back into the smoke-filled kitchen. . . . After that, I became more careful."

It took this mother several months to dismantle the nursery and put her baby's clothes in a suitcase. Other parents refuse to accept the birth certificate (some send it back to the hospital) or open the envelope containing the baby's photograph until weeks have elapsed. Women who have undergone spontaneous abortions may pretend, briefly, that they never were pregnant in the first place. Denial can take numerous forms; *how long it persists* is the critical question.

While prolonged distancing from the event and continuation of normal, nongrieving behaviors suggest a pathologic response, a preliminary period of "shellshock" is not the exception but the rule. Emily Dickinson, who never experienced a tragic outcome of pregnancy, described this early phase of grief with stunning accuracy.

> After great pain, a formal feeling
>   comes—
> The Nerves sit ceremonious, like Tombs—
> The stiff Heart questions was it He,
>   that bore,
> And Yesterday, or Centuries before?
>
> The Feet, mechanical, go round—
> Of Ground, or Air, or Ought—
> A Wooden way
> Regardless grown,
> A Quartz contentment, like a stone—

This is the Hour of Lead—
Remembered, if outlived,
As Freezing persons, recollect the
    Snow—
First—Chill—then Stupor—then the
    letting go—

Anger

"Why me?" "How could God have done this?" "The doctors are all incompetent." Anger follows denial, often overlaps it, and generally continues to be a factor throughout the later phases of bargaining and depression.

"I was furious, with a child's sense of the unfairness of it all," confessed one mother at a group meeting. "I'd done all of the right things, and it hadn't made a damn bit of difference!" "You look at all the unwanted babies, all the battered babies, and you remember how careful you were," added another. "And then you meet a woman who smoked three packs a day during pregnancy and delivered a healthy baby anyway, and you wonder: Why me?"

Life *isn't* fair, yet we sense it ought to be: "I felt tremendous outrage at God, at my husband, at the world. There were times when I became so incensed that I'd beat at the basement walls with an old piece of metal I'd found. The marks are still there. . . ." "There was a scream inside me, wanting to come out. I mainly took it out on the kids, yelling at them and smacking them for things I would ordinarily have tolerated. Somehow, they understood and forgave me. . . ." "I'd been almost hysterically conscientious during pregnancy, because I am diabetic and this was my third try. My blood sugars were perfect. I didn't gain an unnecessary ounce. After I aborted, I had to share a room with another diabetic woman who had done exactly the opposite—eaten brownies and fudge, gained forty pounds—and still given birth to a chubby baby boy. I remember that on my way home from the hospital I stopped at an ice-cream parlor and devoured a hot fudge sundae with whipped cream. Of course, I became terribly ill afterward. But it was my way of striking back at what seemed to me then, as it does today, a colossal injustice."

Guilt and righteous indignation are actually very closely related—the former merely being the direction of anger toward the self, rather than outward. If maternal rage is not worked through in mourning the likelihood is strong that it will turn on itself, in the form of self-destructive behavior and/or chronic depression.

Like the denial-isolation stage of grief, the anger stage serves a valid purpose: to direct some of the aggressive energy released by the tragedy *away* from the mourner at the time when it is most intense, and therefore most likely to be harmful. Having scrutinized her conduct during pregnancy, the bereaved mother searches for additional targets for her rage . . . and finds them in her husband's indifference, the stupidity of the medical profession, and finally Fate, or God.

> It happened to me.
> God chose me.
> Hell knoweth no fury like a woman-in-labor,
>   scorned.
>   —*Marion Cohen*,
>   from "Does Time Heal All Wounds?"

"If we can find someone to blame or some explanation that will enable death to be evaded," says Parkes, "then we have a chance of controlling things. It is easier to believe that fate is indifferent, or rather positively malevolent, than to acknowledge our helplessness in the face of events. . . . Railing against God or Fate is, of course, only another way of trying to control the order of things. It is not so much an expression of helplessness as an attempt to influence events by browbeating their author." [7]

Looking back on her experience as the mother of two older children, Marion Cohen points out: "Kids are always asking 'Why?' 'Why can't I have ice cream?' 'Why can't Amy sleep over?' 'Why did you hit me, Mommy?' No matter how often or how logically you explain it, they're not satisfied. They repeat, 'But why?' The reason they repeat the question so often is because they don't really want to know the answer. What they want is for things to be different. They want to be told, 'Okay, you can have ice cream,' or 'Amy can sleep over,' or 'I promise I'll never hit you again.' It's not curiosity on their part; it's a demand for change. And so with us. 'Why did it happen?' We ask God. But we don't really want to know why. What we want is for God to undo it, to tell us that since there is no acceptable explanation, it didn't really happen."

In a fetal or newborn death the parent is confronted with a loss so profound and seemingly so senseless that even a previously devout believer may have difficulty retaining her faith in God's justice.

> Lord Jesus, where are you? *I'm supposed to know, Lord!* But out there among the "whys" and the hurt and the silence in death—out there, Lord, I feel so all alone and helpless. I look for you in the stiff blue paleness of a dead baby's face—but there's nothing. I seek your face in the falling tear-blood of a grieving mother. She squeezes her Bible—wringing it like a towel—as if somehow, Lord, you will leap from its worn pages with comfort and peace. But there's only the sound of squeaking leather. And suddenly, Lord, the mighty Word is a frail and speechless book—so mute—and we, Lord, are numbed and deaf to its pretentious proclamations. If I were squeezing the book—it would be in anger to choke *you*. Where are you, Lord Jesus? Where are your wounds, deep and red? Not on my speechless lips (mouthing religious nothings born out of my own fears). Where are you, Lord Jesus? I wait to hear your voice—but only the silence remains—Are you really there, Lord—making your strength perfect in my weakness?
> —*John Gordon Anderson*
> FROM "PRAYER—UPON THE DEATH OF AN INFANT"

In the face of bitter reality, the platitudes sound hollow. C. S. Lewis notes that for a bereaved mother the reassurance that her child is with God may be "a comfort to the God-aimed, eternal spirit within her. But not to her motherhood. The specifically maternal happiness must be written off. Never, in any place or time, will she have her son on her knees, or bathe him, or tell him a story, or plan for his future, or see her grandchild."

"What reason have we," Lewis asks, "except our own desperate wishes, to believe that God is, by any standard we can conceive, 'good'? Doesn't all the *prima facie* evidence suggest exactly the opposite?" [8]

Bargaining

> Oh God, please-please *please* turn the
>   clock back.
> And please make me know so I can do things
>   differently.

Please please-oh-please.
I promise I won't ask any questions.
    —*Marion Cohen,*
        FROM "DOES TIME HEAL ALL WOUNDS?"

If God is not innately good, then maybe He at least could be persuaded to make a deal? Unlike the situation of a family confronted by terminal illness, the parents whose child has died before or shortly after birth realize, on the conscious level, that *there are no options.* Nonetheless, the desire to recreate the past is strong, as Marion Cohen suggests. From time to time, the sanest mother finds herself playing "let's pretend." In return for good behavior on her part—for going to church or to the synagogue regularly, for taking her multivitamins, for gaining less or more weight, for swearing off cigarettes—the Divine Plan will be revised in her favor. Only it never works out that way.

(Obviously, bargaining—like anger—is closely tied to maternal guilt. It is mainly those behaviors that the mother suspects may have been damaging to the fetus that she vows to change, if given a second chance.)

Psychologically, the crisis of an unsuccessful pregnancy induces a sense of powerlessness which relegates its victims to the status of dependent children. When a child first learns that the universe, far from being the warm, secure blanket suggested by infancy, is in fact threatening and capricious, he defends himself the only way he can—by pretending an omnipotence, a magical ability to deal with the forces that he senses far outweigh his own. These complex mental mechanisms, or narcissistic defenses, are not unique to childhood; any profound loss or threat of loss may call them into play.

It is hardly surprising that, when faced with a reality so clearly beyond her comprehension, the bereaved mother (1) blames herself ("If only I hadn't taken those aspirins . . . had sex . . . gone skiing.") as though she had power over all of life's uncertainties, and even death itself; and (2) retreats for brief intervals into the child's world of magic, where "wishing makes it so."

Depression

The preliminary stages of grief give way, in very short order, to depression. Frequently this occurs when the mother returns home from the hospital and has to face her normal routines of household management, child care, and/or outside employment once again. "My loved ones were terrific," one woman commented, "but I found I had problems dealing with people who didn't know me so well. Those who were aware I had been pregnant, like the mailman, would automatically grin when they saw me and ask, 'How's the baby?' Then there would be this awful pause before I would manage to get out, 'The baby died.'"

If the baby was stillborn or died shortly after birth and there has been a commemorative service, the real impact of the loss may only begin to be felt after the last guest has departed. Looking back at those days, a mother recalls: "The weekend after the baby died, our house was full of sympathetic people. By late Monday morning, everybody had left and I felt completely abandoned. I told my husband that if he went to the office that day I was going to divorce him."

Some mothers manage to find creative solutions for this problem: "I made what I still feel was a very wise decision, to remain by myself, with only my immediate family around me, until the initial shock had been absorbed. Since I didn't want to lose touch with my friends completely, I asked my mother to call them and tell them what had happened, asking them to please return the call in a few weeks' time, rather than immediately. This worked out very well, with one friend visiting me the weekend after my homecoming, another the following week, several more the week after, and so on. I wasn't besieged by callers, yet I didn't feel that I had been abandoned."

As with other phases of the grief process, responses to depression are highly individual. Some women cannot bear to be alone and plunge into a whirl of professional and social activities as soon as they are physically able: "I couldn't stay at home. The house was too empty. I kept passing the nursery. . . . Even though I still felt a little weak, I had to get out."

Others find comfort in the peace and solitude of familiar surroundings: "I tried to avoid contacts with other people and situations that I knew would provoke awkward questions. My husband wanted me to accompany him to a corporate banquet, and I told him, 'No, I don't want to go, because people will ask about the baby and I'm just not ready to cope with that yet.'"

"The original period of constant wallowing was important to

me," Marion Cohen writes. "I needed to be alone—alone with my husband, alone with my baby, alone with my two other children, alone with my writing, and just plain alone." [9] Colin Murray Parkes points out that there is a characteristic "home valency" which prompts the individual who has lost one source of emotional security to remain close by other havens of safety, either people or places. Thus, a bereaved mother may become more dependent upon her husband and may dread the thought of being left by him, even for short periods. Fears that some terrible harm may befall him or her other children are common and reflect the mother's new perception of the universe as quixotic and dangerous. Other fears (such as panic at seeing menstrual blood) and vivid nightmares about the baby are also fairly common.

In contrast to the bereaved woman's reliance on those closest to her, overtures by casual friends, neighbors, shopkeepers, and others not intimately connected with the event are often unwelcome, especially during the weeks when pangs of grief are at their height. The confusion of voices represents a distraction from the work at hand—from the reality-testing and taking stock of her life which the mother must do in order to find new pathways of hope.

Because those who do not understand her situation will usually try to steer her away from "morbid" topics and from the house itself (at least from the nursery, or whatever portion of space had been allocated for the baby), the mother may respond with irritability or even anger to basically well-intentioned remarks. Or, like the woman quoted previously, she may make a conscious effort to avoid such confrontations by restricting her contacts to family members, close friends, or other members of a support group: "I didn't talk baby-talk to anyone who didn't want to hear it. I just avoided that person's company. It was all I thought about, all I wanted to talk about."

Since, at this stage, mere mention of the loss is enough to provoke tears, the mother is also likely to avoid discussing the subject if she senses that a highly emotional response might embarrass the sympathizer: "Everybody is afraid of saying the wrong thing. No one understands that when you cry, you are really crying because of what happened and not because of anything anybody said."

Unfortunately, among those who often do inadvertently say the wrong thing are the couple's parents. One woman's mother informed her that, by miscarrying on December 24th, she had "ruined Christmas for the whole family." Another woman's mother offered her and her husband financial assistance to adopt a baby, "since it didn't seem likely [they] would have one of their own." (By once again reducing the mother to the status of a dependent child, reactions such as this only confirm her perception of herself as a helpless victim.)

Following an unsuccessful pregnancy, a woman may feel burdened by the need to hide her feelings from her parents: "My folks had always thought of me as being strong and capable. I guess I was unwilling to change that opinion and admit that I felt miserable and defeated." Or, if she decides to be open and share her grief, she may find herself brushed-off with an "I have to go now" or rewarded with a recital of all of the women of their acquaintance who had experienced unsuccessful pregnancies and then proceeded to bear healthy children. Commented one woman: "Mom kept trying to cheer me up with stories about women who had gone through miscarriages and come out with healthy babies. She meant well, but I just couldn't cope with it at that point. What I wanted was acknowledgment of the dismal way *I* was feeling, not other people's success stories."

It is difficult but necessary for a woman to be able to say to her own parents, as she would to a friend whose words of condolence were inappropriate, "I know you mean well but what you are saying only makes me feel worse." Rather than pretend optimism ("You'll feel better in the morning . . . tomorrow . . . next week"), the older woman can then express her *own* disappointment and, by grieving along with her daughter, help the younger cope with her feelings of betrayal and despair.*

"Grieving is a time of selfness," writes Harriet Sarnoff Schiff.[10] What the mother who has experienced a fetal or newborn death needs most of all not only from her parents but from caregivers and the rest of the community is recognition that her self-absorption, her emotional outbursts, her fears, and her fantasies are normal and acceptable behavior for one who has suffered a great loss.

"I didn't like it," recalls Marion Cohen, "when [my mother] told me, once again, all about how tragedy breeds art. I'd been a good

---

* There are, of course, pathological family systems in which feelings of anger and recrimination are much more evident than in the examples cited. If, for example, one set of grandparents has bitterly disapproved of their child's choice of a mate, the death of an anticipated grandchild ("We knew nothing good would ever come out of that match") may dramatically increase the tension between generations.

poet *before* my tragedy, I thought bitterly, and it wasn't art I'd wanted to breed this time. And I didn't want to think about the others, whose tragedies had bred art (like Mahler with his *Kindertotenlieder*), or those whose tragedies *hadn't* bred art. I didn't want to think about the others, not just yet. I wanted to be alone, unique, self-pitying, moody, depressed, and mad." [11]

As weeks pass, the angry or "protest" phase of mourning generally yields to a loss of aggressiveness, apathy, and despair. The acute pangs of grief fade gradually into a dull, persistent ache.

> Reality thumps
> Like a room full of darkness, like footsteps
>   outside
> Reality thumps.
> —*Marion Cohen,*
> FROM "DOES TIME HEAL ALL WOUNDS?"

C. S. Lewis observed that no one had ever told him about the "laziness of grief." Indeed, the slightest effort often seems like too much. "I cooked," said one mother, "but only because I had to, and then only easy recipes that took no thought. I remember we had lots of roast chicken that year. . . ."

There is a tremendous sense of futility: "Nothing seemed to give me pleasure. We planned to take a vacation, but somehow we never got further than the travel agent's office. It just didn't seem right. I knew I wouldn't enjoy it. Everybody said, 'It will make you feel better.' But I didn't want to feel better—I wanted my baby back."

"What good is it?" the mother asks herself. "It" may range from getting up in the morning, to resumption of sexual relations with her husband, to the planting of daffodil bulbs to bloom in the spring: "You see connections everywhere. After the baby died, I realized that my garden, and even my houseplants, had also been unproductive for about a year. It was as though nothing planted by me would ever bear fruit."

The analogy of a barren and unprofitable garden is frequently used by bereaved mothers to express the sense of unworthiness that stems from an unsuccessful outcome of pregnancy. Although some of the early guilt/anger has already been worked through at this stage, the corollary to "What good is it?" is surely, "What good am I?" A young radio announcer explained: "I had always considered myself a problem-solver. Somebody who was able to overcome obstacles. Suddenly, here was an obstacle that I hadn't been able to overcome. I had been unable to save my own child."

"You never stop looking for answers," is a comment heard at meetings of bereaved parents. "Even if you didn't smoke or drink or take drugs," said one woman, "there's always something in the back of your mind to pin the blame on. You think: Maybe it was the time I slipped on the cellar steps? Or: Maybe it was that virus I had in my third month. . . ." "I blamed my husband for not insisting that I stop work during the latter half of my pregnancy," offered another. "And I blamed myself for taking so many analgesics for the migraines I had during that same period. . . ." Added a third: "We had a neighbor, an old woman, who used to watch me hang my clothes out to dry and kept warning me not to raise my arms above my head so much. Well, crazy or not, there were times when I caught myself thinking: Maybe she was right, after all."

"For the most part," says Marion Cohen, "society says and believes that God rewards the good and 'helps those who help themselves.' So it stands, not to reason but to emotion, that if God didn't reward you, you couldn't have been very good."

The loss of self-esteem associated with the baby's death often reminds mothers of similarly humiliating experiences in their past, particularly experiences associated with menstruation, sexual activity, childhood and adolescent body image: "As a teenager, I felt that there was something wrong with me because my periods were so irregular. After the baby died, I thought about that and wondered if perhaps it hadn't been a sign that I wasn't supposed to have children at all."

Gradually, however, the mother discovers that other women echo her concerns; that, although the details of her experience are unique, the fears and guilts and frustrations are not; and that women throughout the ages—and many of her contemporaries—have shared in this common heritage of maternal grief. "I thought I'd never known anyone who had miscarried" the radio announcer continued. "In fact, it turned out just the opposite. Cousins, aunts, friends of mine, my mother's friends . . . all women I thought I knew well. They had lost babies, too, only nobody had said anything."

She contacts or is contacted by a bereavement group and begins to attend meetings. She eats in restaurants, or goes to an occasional movie with her husband. The listlessness dissipates. She feels more alive. *She begins to heal.*

Acceptance

> Hurting seemed to alternate with numbness. Mike returned to work the following week. I stayed home and slept a lot. When I realized I wasn't sleeping so much anymore, and I wasn't totally hurting either, I knew it was time to get back into the world.
>
> —*Connie Purcell*

There are critical turning points in the grief process—some immediately apparent, some that are recognized only with the passage of time. Reconsidering the events that followed her hospitalization, Connie Purcell—the young mother whose diary is presented on p. 92—writes: "It was slow, but our sense of mending grew. It was almost a physical feeling. Not a steady growth, but rather two steps forward and one step back. Seeing pregnant women, women with babies, baby clothes in shop windows—it took quite a while before those things weren't painful.

"Then we had to get through spring. The baby had been due on April 22, and as the end of March approached I found myself dreading the date. I would have liked to skip the whole month. Throughout pregnancy, I had identified with nature. Everything blossoms in the spring, I thought, and our baby will be born in the spring. Now, on my down days, it seemed like a mocking joke.

"Still, on Sunday, April 23, we arranged to have flowers on the altar at church in memory of our little boy. And the next weekend we planted trees and shrubs in our own back yard. It was our way of affirming that life goes on, it cannot be kept down . . . although we only half believed it at the time."

Colin Murray Parkes observes that a memorial service or visit to the cemetery on such an anniversary can have the significance of a rite of passage, indicating that the bereaved are now free—not to forget the dead, but to undertake fresh commitments.

Strong religious ties are certainly an advantage in overcoming the hopelessness of bereavement. The rituals of mourning not only draw the family together and provide community support in time of crisis. They also give the parents a much-needed opportunity to take affirmative action, to do something, if not to prevent the tragedy (since this would be impossible), at least to mark its occurrence.*

Bereaved parents who lack a specific religious affiliation can still exercise the option of conducting a brief, nondenominational memorial service (in the hospital, at home, at graveside following burial or cremation) as a way of saying good-bye. Some couples find that such a service, even years after the event, can bring comfort or, as one mother put it, "take care of the unfinished business." In cases where pregnancy has been cut short by a spontaneous abortion, the couple may wish to plant a tree or make a small donation to charity in memory of the child who did not live.

A funeral or memorial service is, however, only one in a long succession of turning points in grief work. Going back to a previously held job may be another. Marion Cohen returned to part-time teaching six weeks after her daughter's death. She remembers it as a kind of therapy, "but there was a sense of unreality, too. Every so often I would stop in the middle of a lecture and wonder: How can I be doing this?"

Dismantling the nursery and storing or lending out the baby's clothes is usually another milestone. Although it is considered unwise for family or friends to remove reminders of the baby's existence before the mother returns home from the hospital, eventually this must be taken care of. The inability to pack up infant clothing and toys even after several months have elapsed is an indication that grief is not being resolved.

"I lent the baby furniture and most of the clothes to a friend who became pregnant shortly after I did," recalled one mother whose long-awaited first pregnancy ended in a stillbirth. "It wasn't so much that she needed them—although she did. I wanted to be able to associate them with something other than my loss."

The fear that rearrangement of the baby's room or any other "return to normalcy" constitutes an abandonment of the dead is common among bereaved parents. However, the realization that the

* Interestingly, the Judeo-Christian tradition recognizes that an individual's connection with God is put to a strenuous test in the period immediately following bereavement. Rabbi Steven Moss, coordinator of the Jewish chaplaincy service at Sloan-Kettering Cancer Center in New York, notes that Judaism both recognizes that death severs one's relationship with God and makes provisions, through a formalized period of mourning both before and after burial, for a renewal of faith and trust. The grief work cycle in Jewish tradition, Moss writes, entails "the realization that while death eats at one's relationship with God, as the mourner returns to life again his relationship with the God of life and death must also be renewed." [12]

alternative—continued memorialization—is apt to be destructive not only to herself but also to the mental well-being of her husband and surviving children* gives the mother the strength to start picking up the pieces.

> I stare at the ghost of the bassinet.
> My ghost arises,
> Lifts you, holds you, feeds you, smiles
>   at you.
> . . . Do you know I have to forget you
>   for the sake of my other children?
> . . . Do you know I have to get over you
>   for the sake of my love and my life?
> Well, not exactly get over you.
> Just not dwell on you so much.
> Do you know there will soon come a time
> When we can't go on meeting like this?
>   —*Marion Cohen*
>   "Good-bye"

The transition between depression and acceptance is often so gradual that the woman is aware of it only by the absence of previous symptoms: "Mornings used to be the worst. I would think: When I can get through a whole morning without crying, I'll be on my way. And then somehow, it happens, so slowly that you aren't even sure of it at the time. The memory doesn't fade—only the intensity of it."

Recalling how, with the typical guilt of the survivor, she had resisted enjoying any aspect of her life in the weeks after her son Robby died, Harriet Sarnoff Schiff writes: "It was as if my grief served as an umbilical cord to keep him close to me. A part of me. My laughter brought about a sense of 'letting go' and I was by no means ready to let go of him." [13]

When she realized that her occasional lighter moods were an indication of survival, not betrayal, Schiff was able to gradually resume a normal life, accepting occasional social invitations and taking pleasure in the things that had pleased her before her little boy's death: "I was not leaving him alone when I laughed. I could not hold him closer when I cried. He was dead despite what I did or did not do." [14]

* See Chapter 5.

Rabbi Earl Grollman, author of numerous books and articles on helping families cope with death, quotes a Biblical story illustrating the same theme. The firstborn of Bathsheba and King David was critically ill, and the king spent the entire night in fasting and prayer for his recovery. When the infant finally died, the servants were afraid to tell David for fear that his grief would overpower him. The king, however, guessed what had happened, and when his fears were confirmed, arose, washed, prayed, and began to eat. In response to the servants' amazement, David explained: "While the child was yet alive, I fasted and wept; for I said, 'Who knoweth whether the Lord will not be gracious to me, that the child may live?' But now that he is dead, wherefore should I fast? Can I bring him back again?" [15]

Accepting a tragic outcome of pregnancy does not mean that the mother will ever perceive her loss as being reasonable, fair, or just. It is a bow to the inevitable, a recognition that life can be painful and paradoxical—yet life goes on.

> She'll never grow up;
> She'll always be two days old;
> She'll always be a baby;
> *I'll always have a baby.*
> —*Marion Cohen*
> FROM "THE ONE WHO DIED"

4
The Caregiver's Response

My pregnancy was a normal one, but we lost the baby. . . . Death was due to strangulation by the cord. I hemorrhaged ten hours after delivery and went into shock.

Within twenty-four hours a sort of "business-as-usual" attitude prevailed among people around me. . . . In most instances, the baby was not mentioned. The chaplain did not call and no one asked me if he should be asked to visit.

—Joan Marie Johnson, R.N.,
"STILLBIRTH—A PERSONAL EXPERIENCE"

ALTHOUGH THE EXPECTANT parents are clearly the most deeply affected, they are not the only ones who regard a tragic outcome of pregnancy as a personal defeat. For physicians, nurses, and other health workers charged with maintaining the well-being of mother and child, a fetal or neonatal death today comes as a shock—a failure in an obstetrical system no longer geared to accept such failures as inevitable.

And like the rest of society, the medical community's response to an unanticipated death is often one of hasty retreat. By maintaining normal composure (or what passes for it) in the face of parental grief, the caregiver attempts to remove him- or herself from direct involvement. An overwhelming sense of failure and remorse, anxiety about possible criticism by professional colleagues, and, last but not least,

72

fear of litigation may cause the obstetrician to withdraw from all but the most obligatory contacts with the bereaved couple—at precisely the time when they need him most.

THE MYTH OF TECHNOLOGIC INFALLIBILITY

"The intensive struggle for life now practiced in most neonatal units," say Drs. Marshall Klaus and John Kennell, "has some of the spirit of a sports arena, where a 'loss' is almost unacceptable." [1] When death occurs, not only the physician in charge but every member of the obstetrical team is touched by a sense of defeat and the urgent desire to pin the blame elsewhere. Feelings of hostility may not be expressed in words (a member of the nursing staff will rarely come out and tell an obstetrician that his directions were ill-advised, for example), but they can have a palpable effect on team interaction and cooperation. Furthermore, the physician's sense of responsibility, particularly if he is young and relatively inexperienced, may cause him to assume that the parents and/or other staff members will view him as being at fault even when this is clearly not the case.

Anger is a normal component of the response to loss, and it is to be expected that bereaved parents will, in addition to blaming God, fate, and themselves, direct some of their hostile feelings toward the physician and nursing staff. "From the earliest times women have sought help from medicine men, experienced elderly women, midwives, down to the present skilled accoucheurs," observes Andrew Elia. "Whatever person was chosen to be by her side became an important instrument for her safety, prized above earthly possessions. Today the obstetrician assumes a more profound role and an even greater responsibility. His work has been dramatized because of the advances in medicine and because of his superior training; the laity expects perfection of him. If the outcome is a happy one, there is rejoicing and affirmation of faith and trust, but if the result is unfavorable, the close relationship between the doctor and patient may be severely strained. We have nobody to blame but ourselves for this situation, because we have reported our victories but have not had the courage to spell out our limitations and shortcomings." [2]

It has been suggested that today an unspoken contract exists between the obstetrical patient and her physician. For her part, the patient promises to follow instructions: to eat sensibly, obtain adequate rest, take any additional precautions that may be recommended in view of her medical history, and schedule regular prenatal appointments. In return for her cooperation (for being a "good" patient), the obstetrician and staff agree to deliver a healthy infant—preferably by the vaginal route.

Obviously, this is an unrealistic projection, for however advanced we may be technically, the battle can still be lost. Regardless of how sharply the perinatal mortality rate drops, there will always be instances in which the contract cannot be satisfied. Nevertheless, adds Elia, "the relationship [between doctor and patient] need not be dissolved; grief need not become destructive, provided that the obstetrician shares in it, shows compassion and meets hostility in the open field." [3]

It is noteworthy that parental anger and resentment are generally *least* when the following conditions apply: (1) the parents are kept informed of their baby's progress and permitted to take part in critical decisions regarding withdrawal of life support and other issues of care, and (2) physicians, nurses, and other staff members allow their human compassion to surface and, instead of turning away from the family, openly display their own sadness.

J. Cullberg observes that the bereaved mothers in his Stockholm study were extremely sensitive to every nuance of their physician's response, including facial expressions and other forms of "body language." Ronald Knapp and Larry Peppers report that well over half of the mothers in their survey perceived the doctor as being "insensitive, aloof, and unconcerned." [4] Whatever relationship may have existed between the couple and the obstetrician prior to the baby's death was often abruptly terminated, as the following examples illustrate: "I haven't been back to the obstetrician who handled my delivery. He seemed so casual about the whole thing. . . ." "My husband and I felt strongly that I should change doctors. Going back to the same group would have been like returning to the scene of a crime."

Rather than being viewed as a natural disaster, the death of a fetus or newborn is seen by twentieth-century observers as a "crime" in which both parents and health professionals are implicated. The idea that certain deaths may be inevitable is unacceptable to Western culture and *particularly* to physicians.

"It is true, as everyone says these days, that doctors do not know what to do about death. . . ." writes eminent physician-author Lewis Thomas. "What is not so generally recognized is that doctors, especially young doctors, are as frightened and bewildered by the act of death as everyone else. When they avert their eyes it is not that they have lost interest or find their attendance burdensome, because wasteful of their talents; it is surely not because of occupational callousness. Although they are familiar with the business, seeing more of it at first hand than anyone else in our kind of society, they never become used to it. Death is shocking, dismaying, even terrifying. . . . It is the most unacceptable of all abnormalities, an offense against nature itself." [5]

Denial is applied most vigorously of all to the commonest form of pregnancy loss: spontaneous abortion. With the excuse that couples generally find a miscarriage easier to deal with emotionally than a late fetal or neonatal death ("But," as one mother retorted angrily at a parents' group meeting, "who's counting?"), many physicians still counsel their patients to "go home and forget the whole thing." The difficulty of mourning a death about which one may have ambivalent feelings, or a love object which is neither fully oneself nor fully individual, is rarely take into account.

A miscarriage, says Jack Stack, M.D., a psychiatric/family health practitioner in Alma, Michigan, tends to be regarded as a minor medical event, "as routine as drawing blood." The emotional overtones that a spontaneous abortion may have for a particular woman—the doubts cast on her reproductive capacity and her femininity, the tendency to search for a justification for punishment within herself or her partner—are seldom recognized by caregivers. Instead, the mother is told to view the episode intellectually, as a reminder that nature weeds out deficient genetic material. Apparently the implication that the woman has, either once or repeatedly, produced an embryo which was unfit for human life is not taken seriously during the gynecologic consultation . . . except by the mother herself: "The day I was told that my second pregnancy had 'terminated,' I reacted by bursting into tears and running out of the gynecologist's office. At my next visit, I was told by this same physician that he and his staff had been very disappointed by my 'emotionalism.' I was, they felt, too intelligent a woman to react so strongly to the loss of a child I had never even felt kick. Well, let me tell you, your intellect has nothing to do with the way you react!"

The very words "termination of pregnancy," "fetal wastage," "abortion," even "miscarriage" are horrifying to many bereaved mothers. (Even the word "loss" is sometimes construed as an avoidance of the real issue, namely, that death is death irrespective of the baby's gestational age.) The medical jargon is not merely depersonalizing. It suggests a sweeping, negative categorization which is particularly painful and demoralizing to the woman who has tried numerous times, always without success, to bring a pregnancy to term: "I remember my hospital card being made out. On one side they typed my name. Across from that, the word 'diabetic.' And right in the middle of the card, in red letters, the words 'habitual aborter.' That's me, I thought. That card is my identity."

THE EMOTIONAL "EXIT" DOOR

"Physicians tend to avoid suffering parents," says St. Louis obstetrician Yasuo Ishida, "not because we do not care, but because we do not know how to approach them. We grieve with them, but do not always understand how to help them effectively." [6] The clinical detachment so prized by those in the helping professions is in part a defense, a way of exposing the professional to manageable doses of anxiety and human suffering. Many doctors and nurses are afraid that if they let down their guard and appear anything other than cool and competent: (1) their show of grief will only intensify the parents' distress, (2) the parents may decide that some technical error on the caregiver's part was responsible for the baby's death, or (3) they will identify so deeply with the sorrow and helplessness of the families in their care that ultimately they will become depressed, bitter, and unable to function effectively. The popular term for this latter phenomenon, well-known to members of all of the service professions, is "burnout."

"Our experience suggests that the opposite is true," says certified nurse-midwife Ruth Wilf of the Booth Maternity Center in Philadelphia. "The parent who sees that the medical staff is suffering along with them will instinctively trust that everything possible was done to save the baby. There are always situations in obstetrics when you look back and think, perhaps I might have done otherwise. But all that anyone—the parents included—really expects is that you do the best that you can with the information at hand."

Midwives at Booth receive extensive training in both the clinical management of fetal and newborn death and care of the parents.

(For more about the Booth program, see page 91.) Rather than withholding emotion, the midwives' attitude is that parents actually benefit from seeing that the caregiver not only grieves with them, but is able to perform her medical duties unhesitatingly despite a significant personal involvement in the loss.

"You don't have to be evasive and try to shield the patient from pain," observes Yale's Raymond Duff. "The pain is there. You didn't cause it, and you will be much more helpful to the family if you just allow them the dignity of their response." People facing a loss of this magnitude really have enormous strengths, the pediatrician adds. Rather than capitalizing on this by encouraging them to handle their grief in their own way—with flexible hospital policies and as much staff support as can be made available—doctors too often take the paternalistic role. They try to exclude the mother, in particular, from difficult and painful aspects of decision-making, and take full responsibility for what really should be a joint effort.

Along with many other institutions, Yale-New Haven Hospital is now beginning to educate its interns and residents in dealing with death and counseling bereaved families, but there are problems. "Role models for engaging in successful discourse about these issues aren't very common," Duff explains. "Most medical school professors are basically technologists. Their concerns are about diseases and bodies and beds. Asking them to train students in areas for which they themselves received no training may be asking too much."

The solution at Yale and many other institutions has been to implement an interdisciplinary approach, enlisting the aid of nursing instructors, psychologists, social workers, chaplains, and other specialists to introduce discussion of death and the problems of the bereaved into the medical school curriculum.

But nurses, and even chaplains, are not immune from burnout either. Frustration, bitterness, and turnover of staff in the neonatal intensive-care unit run high, as they do in other critical-care areas of nursing. Furthermore, until quite recently nursing students, like medical students, received very little guidance for dealing with the special needs of bereaved parents. The expectant mother's deep attachment to her unborn child was rarely touched upon in textbooks. Urged to take a "positive" approach, a nurse might affect a cheerful briskness as she entered the mother's room, ward off questions about the baby's physical appearance or details of the delivery, and generally downplay the importance of the loss with comments like: "It was lucky that the baby didn't survive, with those abnormalities," or "You're young; you can have other children."

As a result, although some mothers can recall in detail, even years afterward, the kind words of a particular nurse assigned to their room, the majority of comments are less favorable. The nurse was "cool and businesslike," "avoided talking to me," or "sounded phony." One mother poignantly summed it up: "She said how sorry she was, but in a monotone. She didn't *seem* to grieve at all. Maybe it just wasn't in the job description."

Within the clergy, as within the medical profession, responses to fetal and newborn death are highly individual. There are hospital chaplains who are equipped to deal with another's loss because they have accepted their own responses to death and bereavement, and there are others who withdraw from contact with the mourner or offer glib responses punctuated by automatic quotations from Scripture. Just as the physician or nurse may hide behind medical jargon and professional detachment, the clergyman may hide behind the convenient umbrella of "God's will."

The Reverend Ronna Case, emergency-room chaplain at Christ Hospital in Oak Lawn, Illinois, writes: "After a while those of us who work in hospital areas where the drama of stillbirth intrudes let presuppositions about 'proper procedure,' 'God's will,' and perinatal death become routine and unexamined. Attitudes become fossilized. What this means is that we really refuse to think about and participate in stillbirth as particular women open up to us." [7]

Although the death of a child is almost invariably followed by some sort of crisis of faith, a woman may be told by the hospital chaplain or her own pastor that her doubts are sinful. "Don't cry, pray" is a common admonition—as though one excluded the other. To a mother who already sees God as a wrathful avenger, the suggestion that her tears will not be forgiven only intensifies her anger and distrust.

According to Case, one Chicago hospital offers the option of a committal service which is performed in the pathology lab *without parents present*. Such insensitive handling of an occasion which ought to have considerable spiritual meaning is troubling, she points out, not only because the primary mourners are excluded but also because of its definite emphasis on "funeral dimensions" as opposed to "birth dimensions." Parents need to be reminded of the connection as well as the letting-go, says the chaplain, who advocates that simple, individualized services be drawn up based upon dialogues with the parents and common tradition. Later pastoral visits can promote grief work by providing suitable "occasions for remembering" the baby's birth and death.

MEETING PARENTAL NEEDS

In the previously discussed study from Sweden supervised by J. Cullberg, investigators observed three different (negative) ways in which hospital staff handled the anxiety provoked by fetal or newborn death: (1) avoidance of the situation, (2) projection of personal anger or guilt onto the patient, and (3) denial or "magical repair" (for example, suggesting to the mother that she conceive another child as quickly as possible). Keeping these points in mind, we'll use the remainder of this chapter to take a closer look at what constitutes typical maternity care for a mother whose baby has died at or before term. We'll also cite some positive examples of management—hospitals where caregivers, rather than brushing aside parental needs or feeling overwhelmed by them, attempt to meet those needs creatively, with the aid of flexible protocols and staff support.

Avoidance

> Nobody ever gets her episiotomy sewn up as quickly as the mother of a stillborn.
> —*Saying among obstetrical nurses*

Often the medical situation directly preceding a fetal or newborn death is an emergency crisis requiring quick action on the part of physician and staff. There may be little time to confer with the parents, beyond a brief description of the problem and the steps being taken to overcome it. Afterward, however, it is the primary physician's responsibility to explain the cause of death as clearly, carefully, and compassionately as he can.

Following a stillbirth, the obstetrician may have little time to arrange his thoughts; nonetheless, it is important that he say *something*, rather than wait for a nurse to speak or allow the deafening silence in the room to speak for itself. Nurses Pauline M. Seitz and Louise H. Warrick vividly describe the situation of one mother, awakening from anesthesia after delivery: "I understand the meaning of the term dead silence. I kept asking, 'Is the baby dead?' No one would answer me and finally a very small voice said, 'yes.' " [8]

Parents whose babies survive birth but die some hours or days later in the intensive-care nursery often complain of having been misled by falsely optimistic reports of the infant's condition. If there has been an adverse indication, the pediatrician or neonatologist should advise the parents of this and keep them informed of new developments as these occur. As one woman said, "It was terribly important to feel that we knew what was happening *at the time* it was happening. Other couples [in the parent's group] told us how awful it felt not to know, or to discover that their baby's condition had actually been deteriorating during the time they expected his condition to improve."

Knowing that the baby is in danger allows the parents to comfort one another and prepare themselves emotionally for a potential loss. Such "anticipatory grieving" has been shown to improve the prognosis for a healthy outcome of mourning. Similarly, parental participation in the decision to withdraw respirator support when prospects of infant survival appear hopeless and close contact with the baby during the final hour(s) of life have been shown to reduce parental feelings of helplessness and promote acceptance. *Despite these findings, most institutions do not regularly encourage parents to participate in critical-care decisions.*

Once the outcome is known, the physician who wishes to flee wordlessly can find plenty of excuses for doing so. Classic exit lines include: "I don't know what to say," and "The parents are too upset to understand anything right now."

It is clear that even saying "I don't know what to say, except that I'm sorry this happened," is preferable to saying nothing at all, especially if the words are accompanied by a physical gesture such as placing an arm around the parents' shoulders or squeezing the mother's hand. One woman, who suffered a spontaneous abortion at four months followed, a year later, by the birth of an anencephalic child, said that her doctor's visible distress as he transmitted the news kept her from emotional collapse. "If he had walked out of the room then, I would never have stood it," she recalls.

The difficulty of interpreting medical information while the family is numbed by shock may be partly resolved by transmitting the essential data immediately, and then repeating or amplifying it in the course of later counseling sessions. If an autopsy is to be performed, the parents should understand the reasons for this (establishing the cause of death; identifying genetic malformations and other problems which may affect the planning of future pregnancies) before signing the consent form. Physicians, midwives, and nurses should indicate readiness to answer any questions the couple may have regarding the completion of birth and death certificates, naming the baby, arrangements for burial or cremation, or use of the hospital chapel for religious services.

When transmitting the results of an autopsy report, it is important that caregivers speak plainly. Medical jargon, clichés, and purposefully vague messages are useless and likely to confuse, rather than reassure, the parents. (For example: "Your baby had an abnormality which was incompatible with life." *What* was the abnormality? *Why* was it incompatible with life?)

In a study of physician followup conducted by Ronald I. Clyman, M.D., and colleagues at the University of California, San Francisco, and Mount Zion Medical Center, only seven out of twenty-six mothers interviewed after perinatal death were completely satisfied with the information they had received from their physician. Ten mothers were partially satisfied, and nine were totally dissatisfied. The investigators noted "a direct correlation between the degree of dissatisfaction and the mother's lack of understanding and/or her morbid grief response." [9]

Seventy-six percent of the total study population of 108 families chose to have hospital followup in the weeks after hospital discharge. However, when responsibility for maintaining communication was left up to the physician, only one-half of the families were ever contacted again following their infant's death.

As a consequence of the Clyman team's investigation, Mount Zion now utilizes a social worker to maintain continuing communication with bereaved families. Parents are routinely seen one to two months after the death in an interview attended by a physician, the nurse most intimately involved in their baby's care, and the social worker. Problems faced by families following a tragic outcome of pregnancy are discussed and further referrals made, as necessary. Contact with a physician in the months following the death has "resulted in better parental understanding of the cause of death and risk of recurrence as well as increased satisfaction with the information received." [10]

One hospital which has pursued a particularly enlightened program since 1974 is the State University of New York's Downstate Medical Center in Brooklyn. The perinatal bereavement clinic, made up of volunteers from the departments of psychiatry, obstetrics, pediatrics, nursing, and pathology of Downstate and its affiliate, Kings County Hospital Center, provides continuing support for parents from the moment the outcome is known, whether death occurs during pregnancy, at delivery, or within the first thirty days of life.

Founded by Lewis M. Cohen, a psychiatrist now at Tufts University, the bereavement clinic was designed to meet the needs of Downstate's varied patient population "ranging from welfare mothers to doctors' wives." Parents are discharged with the telephone number of the clinic's twenty-four-hour answering service and an appointment card for a four-week followup consultation. Older children, grandparents, and other relatives are encouraged to attend this session, where discussion may range from the implications of the autopsy results (if there has been an autopsy) to the effect of the loss on the couple's relationship with one another and their private feelings concerning the baby's death. Staff members report that most families can cope adequately with the crisis given only a minimal amount of help—two or three counseling sessions, at most. Should more intensive guidance be needed, however, other sources in the medical center are always close at hand.

An additional function of such a "bereavement team" is to provide a model of effective management for other staff members. Drs. Marshall Klaus and John Kennell point out the value of such models when they advise that an experienced physician accompany young doctors during their first confrontations with bereaved parents. Observing that no intern or resident would attempt to insert a catheter for the first time without instruction, the Cleveland pediatricians suggest that the presence of a knowledgeable superior gives the younger physician confidence in probing delicate issues and helps identify his strengths and weaknesses in handling parental concerns.

After a fetal or newborn death, the pediatricians advocate that a minimum of three meetings be arranged: the first, directly following the event; the second, two to three days afterward; and the third from three to six months after the baby's death.

Initially, the mourning process can be described to the parents in general terms. The physician explains that they may experience waves of sadness, along with pains in the chest or other symptoms, which will gradually diminish over a period of about six months. During this time, the couple should expect to feel guilty and/or angry at one another and outsiders—reactions which are perfectly normal under the circumstances.

The second meeting provides an opportunity to go over the same material in greater detail, now that the parents have had some time to absorb the news and have begun the grieving process in earnest. The physician should emphasize the importance of keeping lines of communication open, so that misunderstandings between partners are minimized and each feels free to confide disturbing emotions in the other.

Arrangements for a third followup meeting can be made at the close of the second interview. (Klaus and Kennell consider this additional conference so critical that couples who break their appointments are called by the pediatric office and asked to reschedule. About one-half of parents are initially reluctant to return to the hospital, the investigators report, but "they usually seem relieved once they do come.") Autopsy data are reviewed at this time, and the physician checks that parental grief has begun to abate and that obvious signs of distorted or pathologic mourning are absent.

Special attention is directed to any surviving siblings. How are they handling the loss? Would they benefit from referral to a child guidance worker? If the parents have been encouraged to release some of their strong feelings and have been open with and available to their other children, a good outcome is reasonably predictable. On the other hand, the pediatricians note that every year a small number of families do experience pathologic grief reactions and are referred accordingly.

Hostility

Because the care of a small premature infant demands close supervision and numerous physical contacts, nurses in the neonatal intensive-care unit may develop strong feelings of attachment toward their charges and suffer pangs of grief alternating with moods of denial and anger when the connection is severed by death. Like the parents, staff may also harbor accusatory feelings, particularly if there has been some suspicion that the prospective mother neglected her part of the "contract." (For example: an alcoholic or drug-addicted mother; a diabetic mother who has not kept her diabetes under good control; a teenaged unwed mother who openly admits relief over the outcome.)

Nurses in critical-care areas are often frustrated by having to deal, day in and day out, with conditions which are beyond their control; they are disillusioned by the brusque, tactless, and occasionally inept instructions of physicians; they frequently suffer from lack of sleep; they are, as a rule, overworked and underpaid.

Where can the nurse take her anger? Anne Scupholme, director of the nurse-midwifery service at Jackson Memorial Hospital in Miami, writes: "Rarely do nurses feel comfortable in admitting the need for help, or finding it from a professional, on an individual basis. Later, who is available when she needs to cry or scream in order that she can still be of assistance to the family? Where can she go? What happens to her, her family, and to the medical team if she cannot 'let go' at some point?" [11]

The nurse's traditional role requires that she contain her negative feelings. As the comments of bereaved mothers make clear, however, staff frustration and bitterness frequently resurface in inappropriate remarks, or in the nurse's total preoccupation with technical aspects of care at the expense of the mother's emotional needs. The cumulative effects of this "emotional straitjacket" can also be seen in the prevalence of interdepartmental bickering and the high turnover rate among critical-care workers at many large institutions.

Luckily, some hospitals are beginning to recognize the need of nurses for peer support and are instituting weekly or monthly staff meetings to stimulate interdepartmental communication and cooperation, boost morale, and improve patient care. Like the groups for bereaved parents, these discussion meetings help members of the health team identify their feelings and discover that their responses are not unique. Staff are encouraged to explore the relationship between personal attitudes and caregiving and to consider the effects of each nurse's contribution on the function of the team as a whole.

Susan Yates, supervisor of the maternity unit at Chester County Hospital in West Chester, Pennsylvania, suggests that nurses take advantage of taped interviews with bereaved mothers to acquaint themselves with maternal anger and other manifestations of the grief process. Yates notes that as a result of information gained from listening to the tapes during weekly discussion meetings, staff nurses and ancillary personnel become more at ease, spend more time chatting with bereaved parents, and are better prepared to respond to questions related to hospital forms and burial arrangements.

Scupholme offers an additional, practical suggestion for improving the ability of staff to cope with fetal and newborn death: Have nurses assigned to well-patient areas for at least one and preferably two days a week. Occasional relief from the strain of having to contend with overwhelmingly difficult and painful situations, the nurse-midwife suggests, would dramatically improve the nurses' staying-power. "While this plan would need more qualified nurses initially," she adds, "the amount of time, money and energy that is currently wasted in training critical-care nurses could be drastically reduced and the quality of care improved." [12]

Denial of Reality

> I was unconscious during the delivery, so I didn't see the baby being born or anything. The nurse told me afterward that the cord had gotten wrapped around his neck. But I'd seen this television show about infants being sold for adoption, and I had a crazy idea that maybe they'd stolen mine, because he was so perfect, and they were just telling me he was dead. So I asked to see him, but they said, no, that would be impossible. Finally, I got so desperate that I tried to slip down to the morgue, just to see whether I could find him.

The voice above is that of a young woman whom we'll call Carol. The stillbirth she describes was the second in an obstetrical history that included five unsuccessful pregnancies since her marriage at age fourteen. Referred to a psychiatrist upon discharge from the hospital, Carol was diagnosed as manic-depressive and placed on a maintenance dosage of Lithium, a powerful mood-altering drug. During the year in which she remained under his care, Carol's psychiatrist never admitted that her symptoms, which included bouts of unexplained crying and paralyzing anxiety attacks, were in any way related to her pregnancy history. "I guess," she comments ruefully, "he didn't think that losing a baby or two was an appropriate reason to get depressed."

Happily, Carol's story has a positive ending. A concerned nurse-clinician who understood the heartache of pregnancy loss, having undergone several herself, gave her the incentive to change psychiatrists—and get herself off Lithium. With better medical management (Carol is a diabetic), she was able to give birth, about three months prior to our interview, to a healthy baby boy.

Carol's is certainly an extreme case. But it effectively dramatizes the negative impact of a number of standard hospital procedures applied to parents who have undergone a fetal or newborn death. Notice that the mother was heavily anesthetized for delivery, and as a consequence had no recollection of her infant as he appeared immediately after birth. She then was denied access to her baby and her frantic search for him (the normal desire of the mourner to "find" the "lost" object) construed as aberrant behavior. The psychiatrist to whom she was referred apparently had little experience in working with bereaved persons, for he simply acted upon the superficial evidence of Carol's depression without probing the cause. The medication he prescribed—in addition to being inappropriate for the dramatic but transient symptomatology of acute grief—might have been less than ideal had a new pregnancy been conceived. (Lithium therapy in pregnancy is thought to be associated with a rare form of congenital heart disease known as Ebstein's anomaly.)

In fact, until the nurse-clinician stepped into the picture, at no point in the therapeutic process had an attempt been made to supply this patient with what she really needed: factual information about diabetic pregnancy, trained, sympathetic listeners, and reassurance that a tragic outcome was *certainly* "an appropriate reason to get depressed."

Unfortunately, despite all that has been written on the subject, in many institutions rigid regulations and equally rigid or misinformed hospital personnel persist in denying reality when a fetal or newborn death occurs. By both their attitudes and their actions, caregivers may encourage parental avoidance, rather than confrontation, of the issue.

Overuse of medication—during labor and delivery, in the recovery period, and even after discharge—is a common example. Several reports suggest that physicians tend to be overgenerous when prescribing pills for the insomnia and depression that accompany bereavement, probably to relieve their own feelings of helplessness and inability to counsel and console the mourner as much as to relieve the patient's symptoms. Drugs are necessary sometimes, of course, but in general it is better for bereaved parents to brood about and even lose sleep over the experience, rather than suppress it.

Use of anesthesia when a stillbirth has been confirmed is similarly controversial. Although the obstetrician is likely to encourage maximal pain relief out of a sincere desire to help the patient, this may not always be the wisest course. Like Carol, many women who were asleep or even groggy during delivery wish afterward that they had clear memories to fall back on. There is so little confirmatory evidence of the birth that, even if shown the body afterward, the mother may feel dissociated from the event, and from the baby as well. "I discovered that although I respected my obstetrician, I was reluctant to take his word for what happened," lamented one woman who had requested, and received, pain medication. "I guess the mind demands proof."

Then, too, many mothers who have taken a Lamaze or other prepared childbirth course have looked forward to sharing the birth experience with their husbands. One woman commented that going through labor together as planned "made us really a family; even if our little girl couldn't live, we had given her that." Although responses are highly individual, it is likely that anything that alleviates the mother's feelings of powerlessness and contributes to her sense of self-worth is valuable for those reasons alone. "At first I was afraid to hold the baby," another woman admitted, "but when I saw him in the midwife's arms I realized how much I really wanted to. So we held the baby, my husband and I, and we kissed him and counted fingers and toes just like other parents. And he looked perfect, just perfect."

Thanks to the work of Klaus and Kennell and others, the importance of confirming the reality of a stillbirth or newborn death by encouraging the parents to touch and hold their baby has begun to be appreciated. Although many institutions still enforce the old policy of rigid separation, it is becoming increasingly customary for a nurse-midwife or obstetrical nurse to bring the infant to the parents, wrapped in a receiving blanket, for them to hold, examine, or photograph if they wish. Even though the encounter inevitably brings pain, it also resolves the mother's search by providing her with an "outside" baby to take the place of the one she has carried (see Lewis, p. 41).*

"People will not reject ultimately something they have seen with their own eyes," writes Harriet Sarnoff Schiff.[13] Unlike Carol, a

---

* It is unlikely, however, that the search can be fully resolved at this early stage. The finality of death is acknowledged, if at all, only over time.

mother who has had the opportunity to watch her baby being born and/or hold him after death will be spared the nightmare of wondering what he really looked like, or whether perhaps he might have been stolen by the staff in order to cover up some dreadful medical misjudgment.

The amount of contact required can range from a few moments to a few hours. Some parents prefer to be completely alone with the child; others will request that a nurse-midwife or other staff member remain.

Because parents may be too shocked and hurt immediately after the birth/death to consider the alternatives available to them, Christine Stiefel-Conta, a perinatal nursing specialist at The New York Hospital-Cornell Medical Center, advises that they be given plenty of time to think things over and a supportive staff member to stay with them if they wish it. "We emphasize that in our clinical experience, contact with the child is ultimately therapeutic," says Conta. "We stress that parents who elect *not* to see their babies often have second thoughts afterward. But then we add, 'The decision is yours.' "

The birth of a severely malformed child presents staff with a clearly problematic situation. A few years ago, there would have been no question of the decision, as this mother's grim memory illustrates: "I can remember lying on the delivery table for what seemed like an eternity. Finally, the doctor came over and told me the baby had died. I asked to see him, but they told me he was hydrocephalic and I was better off not knowing. For years afterward, I had nightmares about a headless horseman, galloping along a seashore with a grotesque head under his arm."

Today, however, it is believed by most authorities that the fantasy is always more frightening than the fact, and that a parent will find in even a badly deformed child some familiar or especially lovable feature to remember. The entire body need not be exposed; even hugging a fully wrapped bundle gives comfort. Raymond Duff suggests that if parents want to say a final good-bye to their child after autopsy, the body may be brought, covered in a blanket, with only the head and the extremities exposed. As long as the parents are carefully prepared for what they will see, says Duff, "an uncoerced choice for participation is extremely unlikely to bring a bad result."

As an alternative to viewing the baby, the hospital can offer the parents a photograph of the infant, as would be the case with a live birth. Elaborate equipment is not necessary. A simple Polaroid camera, kept loaded and accessible, is sufficient. A couple may not choose to be shown the photograph immediately, but they should know that it is there, in the files, for them to preserve or destroy as they wish. Even parents who are initially reluctant to see a photograph are usually thankful that a record of their infant has been kept, and couples who have no such memento tend to remark, at meetings of bereaved parents, that they wish someone on the hospital staff had overruled their early objections and photographed the body anyway. In addition to photographs, bereaved parents may treasure a blanket, name bracelet, footprint, or piece of clothing—any bit of tangible evidence of the infant's existence that the hospital can provide.

When Confrontation Is Too Painful

Finally, there is one area of hospital policy in which confrontation with reality has inadvertantly been *over*stressed—and that is the area of room arrangements for mothers who have experienced a fetal or newborn death. In the past, few hospitals made any attempts to shield bereaved mothers from contact with healthy mother-infant pairs. Feeding time would become an agony, as this mother recalls: "My roommate felt so sorry for me that she asked the nurse to pull the curtains, so that I wouldn't have to watch whenever they brought her baby in to be fed. I felt badly for her—she couldn't enjoy her baby properly with me around looking miserable. When I asked the nurse to transfer me to a different room, her reply was: 'You've got to face it some time, honey.'"

For most mothers, the time immediately following a loss is *not* the best time to face other women happily interacting with their newborns. Feelings are too raw, jealousy and rage almost uncontrollable. "I wanted to steal someone's baby, so help me," said one mother, looking back on her unhappy days on the maternity floor. The difficulty of expressing grief in a stranger's presence and the need to put up a brave front, so that women who were still undelivered would not become frightened for their own babies, were other bitter memories.

Fathers as well as mothers express frustrations over rigid maternity regulations governing visiting hours and telephone calls. Staff confusion—a nurse or aide wondering aloud where a mother's infant was, when "all of the other babies are being fed"—was mentioned by several couples as having increased their distress. (Various investigators have pointed out that bereaved parents find it much easier to cope with the awkward remarks of friends or co-workers who have not learned of the loss, than with similar mistakes on the part of care-givers. The most obvious explanation is that parents view lapses by physicians, nurses, and other health workers as evidence that the medical community would prefer the whole affair swept under the rug. Unfortunately, even when the mother's situation is known, charting of fetal and newborn deaths may be so inadequate that changing shifts of caregivers have difficulty familiarizing themselves with the baby's sex, weight, gestational age, and other details. Thus, staff easily become the target of parental rage—really inspired by the event itself.)

In view of these difficulties, it has become customary at many institutions to transfer the patient to a private room off the maternity floor as soon as the outcome is known. This spares the family the anguish of seeing other parents interacting with their babies and allows the mother the freedom to express her grief however and whenever she wishes. Some physicians and hospital administrators disapprove of this trend, claiming that bereaved mothers are more likely to look upon a transfer as punishment for presumed wrong-doing or proof that they are an embarrassment to others. Ideally, we think a mother should be offered her choice of room arrangements—whether to stay on the regular postpartum floor or be moved else-where. It is probably more critical that she be:

- given a private room whenever possible (at some municipal hospitals, a semiprivate room may be all that is available);
- permitted access to her husband at all times;
- visited at regular intervals by house officers and nurses;
- offered the services of the hospital chaplain and perhaps a perinatal social worker;
- allowed to go home as soon as her physical condition permits.

CAREGIVERS AND PARENTS TOGETHER

If this chapter has a theme, it is that both caregivers and parents have been victimized by the myth of technologic infallibility, which holds that every fetal or newborn death represents a failure, an aberration, a breach of contract—a crime. So long as we adhere to this view, a degree of distrust (or outright hostility) between the providers and the recipients of care is probably inevitable.

However, there is an alternate side to this gloomy picture, as exemplified by the work currently in progress at Downstate's perinatal bereavement clinic and a scattering of similar programs throughout the country. By enlarging their understanding of the crisis of unsuccessful pregnancy and working actively with bereaved parents, physicians, nurses, and other health workers can promote gradual resolution of grief and make a significant contribution to the mental health of the families in their care.

One institution which has adhered to this philosophy almost since its inception is Booth Maternity Center in Philadelphia. In the intimate setting of a small, family-oriented maternity hospital, Booth's parenting director, Dr. Nancy Johns, and Laurie Rendall, a certified nurse-midwife, head a grief process group which, twice monthly, explores the emotional needs of Booth parents who have experienced a death in pregnancy.

Because not every couple feels comfortable with the open atmosphere of the group, especially in the beginning, a range of services is offered. The aim, says Johns, is "to help the parents by whatever means they want to be helped." In addition to taking advantage of group meetings, home visits, and telephone support, a bereaved mother may request that a Booth staff member accompany her to her postpartum checkup or refer her to appropriate literature on the subject. (The parenting department contains a sizable library.)

"The key word," says Booth nurse-midwife Ruth Wilf, "is not sympathy but empathy. We don't inflict ourselves on the couple or make decisions for them based upon our own judgment of what their needs are. We do try to let them know, verbally and by our actions, that we will be there for them when they need us, not just for a day or two but on a continuing basis."

From the moment a tragic outcome is suspected, Booth physicians, midwives, and ancillary personnel rally around the parents, trying in every way they can to prepare them for the difficult transition that lies ahead. The attention is appreciated . . . and remembered:

"I felt as though I were the only patient on the floor. Whatever I needed, I had, usually without even pressing a buzzer. There always seemed to be someone nearby who would stop in and ask, 'Are you okay? Can we get you anything?' "

"The staff didn't hold anything back. When I felt brave, I could be brave. But when I needed a shoulder to cry on, that was there, too."

"Dr. Franklin [Booth's medical director] explained that my friends and family would gather around and be very sympathetic at first, but that eventually they would go on with their lives while I would still be grieving inside. It's very important to tell women that, because otherwise, when a few months have passed and everyone expects you to go on as before, you won't understand why you can't stop dwelling on it, or you'll be angry at them for their shortsightedness, without realizing that they can't know how you feel."

In view of the all-encompassing nature of the Booth program, it seemed appropriate to end this chapter on caregiving with excerpts from the hospitalization diary of Connie Purcell, a young journalist whose first child, a son, died and was delivered at Booth in the twenty-sixth week of gestation. Although every woman's experience is unique, the reader will recognize certain universals—among them, the vividness with which fine details are recalled.

Diary of a Hospitalization*

Monday, January 9. My twenty-sixth week. . . . I remember feeling the baby move as I dressed for work. I loved being pregnant. I even loved the way I looked, despite all the jokes about having to sit farther back from my typewriter in the newsroom. . . . When I got home from work, I realized that I hadn't felt anything all afternoon. Didn't worry too much, though. Babies sleep in the womb, too. . . .

No movement Tuesday or Wednesday.

Thursday, January 12. A.M. By now Mike and I were really concerned. We called Booth early in the morning, and the midwife who took the call said, "You know what this could mean." I said, "Yes." Mike left work at lunchtime and together we drove to the hospital. (We ask ourselves: Would it have made any difference if we'd gone on Tuesday? Could the baby have been saved by a cesarean?)

* All names in these excerpts are authentic and are used with permission of the quoted parties.

P.M. Ruth Wilf tried to find the fetal heart with a Doptone. Mike thought he could hear it a couple of times, but I knew I hadn't. No heartbeat on the electronic monitor either. Dr. Franklin was called in. Mike and I tried to convince ourselves that the baby was just curled up so the monitor couldn't catch the heartbeat. . . . Dr. Franklin placed his hands on my abdomen and tried to bounce the baby a little, but there was no response. Still, he didn't give up hope entirely. The machine could be faulty, he said. So wait a while. Come back on Monday—and bring a suitcase. . . . Mike and I didn't say much. We held each other's hands, and Dr. Franklin clasped our hands in his. There were tears rolling down my cheeks, but I felt numb. Ruth looked as though she were about to cry, too. Dr. Franklin promised us that everyone at Booth would help us as much as they could. We had to start distancing ourselves from the baby, he said, peeling away all of the personality characteristics we'd been attributing to him. In effect, he was telling us to start saying good-bye. . . . Mike and I didn't talk much on the way home, but I remember with incredible clarity the way things looked—the people at the bus stops, the traffic we drove past. It seemed so strange that life went on as usual, when our baby had died. Many times over the next weekend we would stop and think: It doesn't feel real. How could this have happened to us? We're both so healthy. Everything had been going so well. There weren't any answers. . . .

Friday, January 13. My only memory of that day is just staying at home and holding each other.

Saturday, January 14. A.M. I decided to work my usual half-day, because that would be better than staying at home. Mike played racquetball. Real things, normal things—something to give us balance.

P.M. We called our parents Saturday night. We'd thought about waiting until "it" was over, but decided against it. So there we were, eight hundred miles away from our folks, telling them by telephone that their first grandchild hadn't lived. Each of us is an oldest child and the only one married, so we knew that the shock would come especially hard. I remember my mother saying that she wished she could put her arms around us in person. The calls were short, but a great deal of love was communicated in those few minutes.

Sunday, January 15. It was the longest weekend we had ever lived through. At church we prayed for strength and thought: To-morrow, it will be over.

Monday, January 16. A.M. We arrived at Booth around 8:30 with Mike's things as well as mine in a suitcase. The midwives had told us that he could stay with me the entire time, and that meant so much. "Don't be afraid to lean on each other," they said. "You're in this together; you can come through it together." Mike said he would've gone nuts if he hadn't been allowed to stay with me, hadn't known what was going on. . . .

P.M. One more try with the fetal monitor before starting the Pitocin I.V. Nothing. But my body wasn't ready to give up the baby yet, and all the Pitocin produced was a few twitches. Was I still hoping against hope that the machines were wrong? Mike and I had a little room to ourselves—they brought a recliner in for him to sleep on. I remember that it snowed terribly all that day and the next. We watched the cars outside and thought about how strange it all was. The unreality of it. . . .

Tuesday, January 17. A.M. It was decided that I was to have a prostaglandin suppository to get the contractions going. While we waited for them to set it up, we walked down to the nursery. Cou-ples were going in and out with babies in their arms. We were so grateful to have that little room to ourselves. . . .

P.M. The prostaglandin worked. My contractions became very regular—Mike was timing them. One of the midwives showed me how to breathe through them as they got stronger. That night, too, a kind of miracle happened. My Uncle John arrived in Philadelphia on business from his home in Seattle, and came straight from the airport to see us. With both of our families so far away, it was a real gift. He stayed and talked with us all evening, well beyond visiting hours. No one bothered him. . . .

Wednesday, January 18. It felt like we'd been at Booth for-ever. But my contractions were coming closer together now. I recall being wrenched from sleep (they had given me a shot of Demerol) by the sudden knowledge that it was time to push the baby out. . . . I knew that if I let myself think about the fact that the baby was dead, I wouldn't make it, so I just concentrated on pushing and noticing how Mike seemed to be everywhere at once—holding my hand, supporting my head, touching my back with his fingers. I remember repeating, "It's going to be over, it's going to be over." . . . And it was. We had a little boy, just as we'd known we would. The midwives left us alone together with the baby, to say good-bye. I'd been afraid that he would be deformed, but he was perfect. Only so very, very tiny. His arms were long and thin, and his fingers minuscule, but perfect as well. I touched his arm, and the skin felt rubbery. (We later learned that he had been dead for over a week.) There was nothing we could see that would give us a clue to why he had died. I cried. . . .

Thursday, January 19. We went home on Thursday morning. Dr. Franklin told us that we could try to get pregnant again in anywhere from three to six months. Ruth Wilf added that being emotionally ready was as important as being physically ready. (She was right; trying again became a very definite decision, made in the face of fears that hadn't existed before.) . . . Going back out into the world was very eerie. Sure enough, it hadn't come to an end. There was a little more snow, that was all. Only we felt different. . . . A bit of irony: No sooner had we gotten home than a man from Western Union knocked on the door and handed me a telegram. *The Philadelphia Inquirer* had accepted an article I'd written some time back, on the subject of approaching parenthood. "Congratulations. . . ." I wanted to call immediately and tell them not to run it, but Mike said, "Wait a minute. It was true when you wrote it. It'll be true again. Let it run."* So we did. Mike suggested that the cash value of the proceeds be donated to Booth, and the editor agreed. When the article was published, a number of the midwives called to say they'd enjoyed it. . . .

* Mike's prediction proved to be correct. Fourteen months after her initial hospitalization, Connie Purcell gave birth to a healthy baby girl at Booth Maternity Center.

5
Children: The
Forgotten Mourners

—A Simple Child,
That lightly draws its breath,
And feels its life in every limb,
What should it know of death?
    —*William Wordsworth,*
    "WE ARE SEVEN"

HOW DOES A tragic outcome of pregnancy affect the other siblings in a family? Are young children really conscious of death? What is meant by the term, "replacement child"? Can parents, in the weeks immediately following a loss, work with their children to reduce anxiety and improve communication between the generations?

The question of when children first begin to puzzle over death and finally learn to regard it as permanent has exerted a steady fascination for pediatric health workers, psychiatrists, social scientists, and theologians. To understand how a child might view this most threatening of all separations, we must begin with his level of psychological development—in particular how the youngster distinguishes himself from his primary caregivers, his peers, and finally the rest of the world.

Obviously, psychological development bears a strong relationship to chronological age; one would not expect a four-year-old to exhibit the same response as his nine-year-old sister. There are, however, enormous variations in children's prior experiences, as well as in their perceptions of themselves and their abilities to conceptualize. There may also be an enormous discrepancy between the way a particular child feels inside and how he or she behaves *at the time*, with the result that painful questions sometimes surface only months or years after a traumatic event—when the youngster is developmentally ready to ask them.

Although attitudes about death become increasingly involved and sophisticated as the child matures, even the youngest preschooler may be strongly affected by the loss of an anticipated sibling. First, because there are inescapable changes in the adults around him—depression and irritability, self-preoccupation, disregard of previously structured routines such as the washing of hands before meals or tooth-brushing—which are all the more threatening because they are not fully understood. Second, because the child's place in the family has permanently changed. As a consequence of events beyond his control he is now a survivor, and must learn to cope with the complex implications of that role in a readjusted family equilibrium.

As the bereaved parent struggles for understanding and acceptance of the loss, the youngster wonders: "Where do I fit in? . . . Will my parents still love me the way they did before? . . . *Will I die too?*"

HOW YOUNG CHILDREN VIEW DEATH

Human beings begin to come to terms with separation and loss very early in life. The baby in his crib sees his mother leave the room and, not realizing that she will return, cries. Later, the same infant may play a game of peek-a-boo with one of his caregivers, chortling with delight over the rapidly altering states of presence and absence. Gradually, the child learns to tolerate longer separations, until by the age of three or four he is ready for a half-day nursery, play group, or day care facility. By six or thereabouts, most youngsters have mastered their initial fears of abandonment to a degree sufficient to allow them to engage in larger group activities in the more challenging world of elementary school.

The primal fears do not vanish; they are simply relegated to an unconscious level. Since his caregivers have always returned in the past, the youngster reasons that they will always return to feed, clothe, and comfort him. (It should be pointed out that we are talking here of basically healthy and secure children, and not of those who have experienced early multiple losses, parental death, abuse, or neglect, who may have quite a different set of expectations.)

Preschool children appear to have a rather fluid concept of time. Two-year-olds, for example, frequently have difficulty distinguishing their afternoon nap from a night's sleep. Yesterday flows into today, today into tomorrow, and tomorrow into all of the tomorrows thereafter. In addition, very young children have not yet developed the capacity to make fine distinctions between related objects and tend to lump them together under a familiar heading, such as "policeman" for every individual seen wearing a uniform. Since the blue jay perched on the branch outside looks very much like the bird that perched there last summer, the child concludes that it must be the same bird. Viewed this way, all of natural life appears continuous, without beginning or ending. It is thought that most children are incapable of grasping the *finality* of death as the end-stage of all life until about the age of five.

In a well-known Hungarian study conducted in the 1940s and 50s, Dr. Maria Nagy questioned 378 children between the ages of three and ten about their attitudes toward death. The overwhelming majority of three-to-five-year-olds appeared to regard it as a temporary or reversible phenomenon, something akin to sleep. Some children compared it to a journey (from which return is always possible), while others believed that the dead continued to retain a degree of sensory awareness while appearing lifeless (for example, they could hear but not speak).

The impact of television has not reduced this expectation of reversibility, in the opinion of Dr. Robert Kastenbaum, director of psychological research at Cushing Hospital in Framingham, Massachusetts, and editor of *Omega*, a journal of death and dying. In fact, Kastenbaum points out that certain programs aimed at very young children may actually reinforce this concept. "Notice," he writes, "how many temporary deaths are encountered by the characters of a typical animated cartoon within even a single episode. The 'death' itself can be quite convincing—hero or villain is drowned, crushed, dismembered, etc. But an instant later—without explanation and often without loss of a single whisker—the character returns for his next escapade." [1]

Furthermore, since it is usually the bad guy who "gets it" in the end, the child receives the message (later, from countless westerns and police dramas) that death is a punishment for wrongdoing, rather than something inevitable which happens to us all. This fits in quite well with his developing sense of guilt and retribution. When Mommy scolded him in the past, or was irritable or stopped reading to him, it usually meant that he had done something bad. Observing these same behaviors in the wake of a fetal or newborn death, the preschool or primary-school-aged youngster looks for the individual whose misbehavior must have inspired the calamity . . . and seizes upon the most likely suspect: "I could tell that my son, then aged four, was worrying that his obvious jealousy of the new baby might somehow have caused her death. We had a talk about it, and I explained that *all* children resent the arrival of younger brothers and sisters, and that we didn't expect him to love the baby right away; that would have come in time."

As we observed in Chapter 3, magical thinking is not confined to early childhood. Under conditions of extreme stress, the most sensible adult may believe that her own ambivalence toward a pregnancy, or some imagined oversight on her part, was responsible for the termination of that pregnancy. But its *roots* are there, as Ernest Becker brilliantly sums up in *The Denial of Death*.

"What is unique about the child's perception of the world?" Becker asks. "For one thing, the extreme confusion of cause-and-effect relationships; for another, extreme unreality about the limits of his own powers. The child lives in a situation of utter dependence; and when his needs are met it must seem to him that he has magical powers, real omnipotence. If he experiences pain, hunger, or discomfort, all he has to do is scream and he is relieved and lulled by gentle, loving sounds. He is a magician and a telepath who has only to mumble and to imagine and the world turns to his desires.

"But, now," Becker adds, "the penalty for such perceptions. In a magical world where things cause other things to happen just by a mere thought or a look of displeasure, anything can happen to anyone. When the child experiences inevitable and real frustrations from his parents, he directs hate and destructive feelings toward them; and he has no way of knowing that malevolent feelings cannot be fulfilled by the same magic as were his other wishes." [2]

As the child gains a more accurate view of the limitations on his powers, magical thinking fades into the background and is replaced by more realistic perceptions. And through gradual exposure to the life cycles of plants and animals and the deaths of household pets, older relatives, perhaps even a grandparent, he learns from sad experience that the dead do not return. Still, Nagy's study indicated that children between the ages of five and nine characteristically personified death or cloaked it in fantastical form, as a means of removing it from their everyday reality. At this age, death was spoken of as a skeleton, a bogeyman, or an invisible demon who carried others off in the night (again, the possibility that such an end might be avoided through caution and good luck).

Ultimately, however, the child cannot escape the realization that rather than being always the result of accident or malicious intent, death is permanent and universal. By age ten if not earlier, it is generally felt that most children recognize that their parents will someday die, and that they themselves will eventually suffer the same fate. The painful adult process of seeking a meaning for human existence has been set in motion.

OPENNESS COUNTS

> Ring-a-ring o' roses,
> A pocket full of posies,
> A-tishoo! A-tishoo!
> We all fall down.

To the fifteenth-century children who first chanted this rhyme, death was no stranger. Contrary to the expectation of reversibility just discussed, in plague-stricken medieval Europe it was human life which seemed, even to childish eyes, as fleeting as "a pocket full of posies." In order to understand how youngsters respond to a death in the family, it is necessary to consider not only their chronological age and developmental level, but also the social and cultural climate or framework in which they are raised.

"No child should have to deal with the overwhelming experience of bereavement without prior exposure to small doses of ideas and feelings about death," say Gilbert Kliman, M.D., and Albert Rosenfeld, the authors of *Responsible Parenthood*.[3] Yet many modern parents believe it their duty to shield youngsters from precisely those experiences which could strengthen their capacities to deal with unanticipated traumatic events, such as the illness or death of a close family member. Rather than flushing a dead goldfish or turtle down the toilet and immediately buying a replacement, for example, the parent could take the opportunity to discuss why the pet might have died, show the child how still it is, perhaps even arrange a small "funeral" if that is the youngster's wish. The life cycles of plants and insects, the finding of a dead chipmunk or bird by the side of the road, or the death of a distant relative of the child's can provide additional opportunities for discussing death and grief in a relaxed context. Such gradual, "immunizing" doses of stress, say the authors, prepare the child for more serious confrontations with loss in much the same way that vaccination with weakened polio or measles virus creates antibodies which defend the body against future attack by those organisms. (See "Books That Help Children Cope with Death," p. 112.)

Given that much of gynecologic and obstetrical care is confined to large hospitals from which small children are generally excluded, the death of a fetus or newborn is not terribly difficult to conceal—if that is the adult's intention. It is all too easy for caregivers to restrict their explanations to "Mommy has gone on a trip" or "Mommy had to go to the hospital for a few days, but now she's fine." Except that Mommy, far from appearing fine, will in fact seem dramatically different to a youngster familiar with her every gesture and inflection.

The younger the child, the greater the parents' temptation to avoid painful and difficult references to the loss. What harm can silence do, they reason, if three-year-old Ellen knows little or nothing about birth and wasn't looking forward to the baby's arrival in the first place? Once such a decision has been made, however, it becomes increasingly difficult to bring up the subject at a later date. And a child doesn't have to be very old to build up fantasies about her relationship to an expected brother or sister, or feel frightened and guilty about unexplained changes in her parents' behavior.

Studies by noted pediatrician-author T. Berry Brazelton have demonstrated that, as early as the second month of life, infants can detect changes in their mothers' attitudes and become extremely agitated if the parent remains expressionless, rather than smiling or cooing at the baby, for more than a few moments. And those who work with the bereaved on a day-in, day-out basis are unanimous in their conviction that *the separation and pain of death cannot be hidden from children of any age.* Awkward and embarrassed attempts to spare the children, say nurses Carol Hardgrove and Louise H. Warrick, "build walls between parents and youngsters and set a pattern of withholding talk and expression of genuine emotion. This secrecy can cast a lifetime shadow, creating a fear that the child has no permission to explore. Openly airing all things that affect the family gives children permission and help to continue growing. Without such permission, life can be robbed of vitality." [4]

If Mommy is always crying, if she is too preoccupied to look at his drawings or read him stories, or if Daddy seems distant or reprimands him for things that would previously have gone unnoticed, an uninformed three- or four-year-old may well conclude: My parents are angry because they think I'm bad. And if they think I'm bad, then I must be bad. So (1) I'll withdraw, because there is something awful going on here that no one wants to tell me about; (2) I'll misbehave, because I am bad and that is how bad boys and girls gain attention; or (3) I'll regress, because what my parents really wanted was a baby and, anyway, it feels good to suck your thumb and cuddle a blanket when you're sad and lonely.

Not all children respond this way, of course. But it is common for parents and teachers to report significant alterations in the behavior of surviving siblings following a loss in pregnancy. Several authors have additionally suggested that the failure to deal openly with one's children about a loss is one indication that grief is not being handled well. In an article in *Birth and the Family Journal*, Erna Furman comments that parental success in helping surviving children come to terms with bereavement "can be an accurate diagnostic scale in understanding how far a parent has come. If a parent has not been able to help his or her children with some aspects, those are the aspects that the parent himself or herself has not come to terms with." [5]

Why is it so difficult for parents to talk to their children at this time? In addition to their reluctance to frighten the youngsters or burden them with their own grief, many parents are hesitant to bring up a subject about which they themselves are in a turmoil. "How can I tell my daughter not to be angry at God," one bereaved mother asked poignantly, "when I'm angry at Him myself?"

Unable to recall similar conversations with their elders, the couple lack guidelines for discussion. (Notice again, the parallel with sexual repression; just as we need models for honest cross-generational exchanges about sexuality, we need them for honest discussions about death. And unsuccessful pregnancy involves not one but both of these formerly taboo issues!) Physically and emotionally depleted, they find it difficult to summon up the stamina to provide the needed explanations; where a rational response is called for, an emotional response is likely to be forthcoming. As a result, the very efforts which are potentially the most rewarding to the parent in terms of providing comfort and restoring self-esteem—that is, helping a surviving youngster overcome his or her anxiety about the event—seem almost too exhausting to contemplate. "I couldn't stand the responsibility of having to care for another child," explained a woman whose second pregnancy ended in the fifth month. "It seemed so unfair. I was like a child myself, needing others to care for *me*."

In the wide swings of mood that many women encounter in the weeks after hospitalization, feelings toward older children can vary from one moment to the next. "There were times when I was terribly grateful for the distraction Jenny provided," said one mother of her six-year-old, "and other times when I wished she would just vanish, disappear, so that I could be alone with my grief." "My twenty-four-month-old had just stopped taking his nap," another recalled, "and I was furious because I desperately needed to sleep. Neighbors offered to take him so that I could get some rest, but whenever I agreed I would feel even worse. It seemed like that child, too, was being taken from me."

"You scream at your kids because you're so angry," another woman added, "and then you feel guilty because, of course, you're really screaming about something that wasn't their fault. Then you remember all the ambivalent feelings you had at the beginning of pregnancy and you wonder whether the baby didn't die *because you were such a terrible mother in the first place.*" In fact, bereaved parents are often amazed—and upset—by their reactions. Marion Cohen remembers: "I was haunted by the contrast between my two older children—with their strong, individualistic personalities—and the innocence and dependence of the infant I had lost. At times, when one or the other would act up, I would burst into tears, thinking: The baby wouldn't have done that."

The sounds of children, especially preschoolers, at play can also be jarring to a parent who is in mourning for the baby who will never know what it is to build a house of blocks or watch *Sesame Street*. Yet play serves a valuable function in addition to mere discharge of energy. At a time when the youngster's confidence has been severely shaken by his mother's hospitalization and changed appearance, and by the gloom which settled over the household on her return, parental encouragement to play gives the child the message that it is all right to be alive and happy, even in the midst of adult sorrow, and that he is not expected to share the depths of their grief *or even pretend to*. Doll and group play, in particular, allow children to act out their fantasies of death and burial and alleviate some of their anxieties in so doing. "My daughter was fascinated by the pictures of the baby and showed them to her friends," Cohen recalls. "She would act out the birth and death with her dolls, explaining to whoever happened to be around that 'this baby is very sick.' I found it painful to watch, but at the same time I knew that [the baby's death] was an important part of her life, too, and she needed to accept it on her terms."

In *Maternal-Infant Bonding*, pediatricians Marshall H. Klaus and John H. Kennell observe that because mourning is basically self-centered, the parent's need to be alone with his or her own grief is a frequent contributing factor to communication breakdowns following a loss in pregnancy. "In spite of this," the investigators add, "with some encouragement, a mother can usually find the extra ounce of strength to embrace her children and give them some explanation." [6]

ESTABLISHING A DIALOGUE: SUPPORTING ONE ANOTHER IN CRISIS

> Having an older child to care for was a strong incentive to return to the world of the living. Once, as I was preparing for a family outing, I overheard my son say to my husband: "I wish we didn't have to take Mom with us. She cries all the time."

Helping one's children cope with a crisis which directly threatens their own integrity, discussing such difficult concepts as death and the existence of an afterlife in terms a child can understand and accept—these are things which can strengthen family ties and restore parents' respect for their own competence at a time when self-esteem is typically low. And remarkably, despite the intense preoccupation which results from the mourner's need to immerse herself in her grief during the early weeks, bereaved parents do summon up the stamina to reach out to their children.

Touching helps. A very young child may be incapable of understanding the actual complexities of what happened, but he is a good enough judge of parental behavior to recognize withdrawal when he sees it. Hugging a child of any age takes some of the sting out of a serious message and demonstrates, more eloquently than words can, that the family is safely together in the here-and-now.

"At first I was afraid to cry in front of my little boy," one woman told a meeting of recently bereaved parents. "But then I heard him explaining to a visitor, 'Mommy's upset right now. She's crying because the baby died. She'll feel better in a little while.' And I realized that he was learning to be a compassionate human being, and there was nothing wrong with that."

The stiff-upper-lip approach only widens the communication gap between parent and child. Although it is unfair to burden surviving youngsters with endless showers of tears or unrelieved solemnity, it is not damaging but actually enriching for even small children to learn that life can be painful as well as joyous—and that both good and bad experiences can be profitably shared. "We don't make a religion out of it," say Marion Cohen and her husband, Jeff, "but we don't avoid talking about it, either. It's part of our children's lives, just as it's part of ours."

Rabbi-author Earl Grollman points out that whereas few preschoolers require or benefit from lengthy philosophical explanations of death, all benefit from the reassurance that nothing is being hidden from them. Permission to explore further into the matter when they are ready, a reminder that they do not bear personal responsibility for either the event or its aftermath, and the secure knowledge that their parents will continue to be there to pack lunches, bandage skinned knees, kiss them good night, and meet their other physical and emotional needs are what small children yearn for at this time.

A youngster will, in addition, need some reassurance that he is not going to die of the same mysterious malady as his baby brother or sister. Like adults, children tend to respond with greater anxiety to the unanticipated death of one close to themselves in age than, say, to the death of an elderly grandparent. The absence of a clear medical explanation for many perinatal deaths makes the parents' task of educating surviving youngsters all the more difficult.

It may be helpful for the parent to draw a comparison between the older child's good health—as illustrated by adequate birthweight, favorable reports from the pediatrician or school nurse, progress on the growth chart, performance in games and sports, and so on—and the new baby's frailty, as this mother's approach to the problem demonstrates: "When I came home from the hospital, my four-year-old said to me, 'Mommy, I wish the baby could have lived.' That's all she said, but I could tell that she was confused and frightened by what had happened. So I explained that when she was born she had weighed eight pounds, which was a fine weight for a baby, whereas this baby had weighed less than a pound and was too small to live. Then I showed her pictures of the baby, which didn't seem to frighten her, although she knew he was dead."

The words parents choose immediately following a hospitalization can have the effect of either increasing the child's understanding or contributing to misinformation and distrust. "Loss," for example, is a term understood by adults to refer to the painful absence of a love object. When used in this context, the death of that love object is implied. To a small child, however, loss suggests a more temporary condition. Lost toys and stuffed animals are frequently found under beds and in bureau drawers. He himself may have once or twice "gotten lost" in a large supermarket or department store, only to be reclaimed by a distressed parent or guardian a short time later. From the child's vantage point, therefore, a lost sibling may someday be recovered . . . and what will happen to his place in the family then? Similarly, parents who tell their small children that the unborn or newborn baby is "asleep forever" run the risk of setting off a pattern of sleep disturbance in which the youngster (quite understandably) is unwilling to risk closing her eyes.

As a general rule, it is wise to avoid using euphemisms for the word "death" even when the word itself may be only partially understood. Fanciful views of heaven are equally to be discouraged. "Children intuitively pick up fabrications," counsels Nancy Johns of the Booth Maternity Center. "They sense when you are twisting reality for their benefit. Don't mouth platitudes," Johns advises couples attending sessions of the Booth bereavement group. "And try not to simply repeat what your parents would have wanted you to believe. For example, don't tell your child that the baby has become an angel with tiny wings unless you really believe this and can explain your concept of angels to the child's satisfaction." *

In an article entitled "The Theological, Psychological, and Philosophical Dimensions of Death in Protestantism," the Reverend

---

* One impressionable three-year-old, upon being told that her baby brother was "looking down at her," became terrified that he would fall out of heaven whenever it rained "cats and dogs."

Edgar N. Jackson observes that emphasis on romanticized visions of the afterlife threatens the viability of religion as a refuge and a strength for young people. "The effort to reassure a child by false-hood," warns Jackson, "is doubly damaging because when he finds that he has been deceived he feels anxiety not only about the deception itself, but also about the person who is so insecure that he can no longer be trusted to serve as a dependable source of information about the important questions of life." [7]

Clergymen of all denominations who have studied children's responses to death agree that it is not necessary for parents to claim to have all of the answers. It is far better to honestly say to a young child: "There are things which defy human understanding. I myself do not know what happens after death. Perhaps it would reassure us both to talk about it." Or, if the parent feels comfortable discussing death in a more traditional religious context: "The body is only a container or resting place for life, rather than life itself. There is an invisible part of all of us which lives on even after physical death." Telling a youngster that God wanted his baby sister for Himself, because she was so good, too easily leads the older child to conclude that God may want *him* next; or, alternatively, that he can't be very good or otherwise God would have chosen him instead. Elisabeth Kübler-Ross cites the dramatic case of a little girl who, having been told by her family that God loved little boys so much that He took her younger brother to heaven, never resolved her anger at God, which resulted in a psychotic depression when she lost her own small son three decades later.

To promote realistic concepts of death and grief and help the survivor feel a part of his parents' mourning, attendance at a commemorative ceremony, if there is one, is often advised. Prior to the start of such a service, however, small children especially should receive considerable preparation for what they will see and hear. And parents should make certain that there are enough caring adults around to take a child's hand or answer questions, in the event that they themselves are too preoccupied and upset to interpret his signals of need.

If there is no ceremony (as tends to be the case, especially if gestation was not complete), or the child strenuously objects to taking part in a cemetery ritual, he or she can be asked to answer the door for visitors or help with the dismantling of the nursery and packing of the baby's clothes. Of course, when there is a grave to visit, the child may be taken along on later occasions, as well: "After the first visit, I gave my son the choice of whether he wanted to accompany me to the cemetery or not. He always chose to go and felt very proud to be allowed to water and care for the flowers. Of course, he asked a thousand questions, some of which were painful or difficult to answer, such as when a fresh grave was dug right beside ours and a new mound of earth appeared."

REGRESSION AND FEARFUL TALK

> There is a tendency for any complex system (including living organisms and physical chemical systems) to lapse into a state of lesser complexity of organization when damaged. . . . The regression of a frightened child who must be cuddled or even slept with as if he were once more a baby can be a means for acquiring short-term increases of psychosocial sustenance, or valuable in restoring more stable uses of psychological energy in a short period of time.
> —*Gilbert Kliman,*
> PSYCHOLOGICAL EMERGENCIES OF CHILDHOOD

Under the stress of a sibling's death, surviving youngsters may lose interest in schoolwork or display uncharacteristically loud and aggressive behavior toward their peers. More commonly, especially when the death is that of a helpless infant, the older child will regress to an earlier stage of development and by thumb-sucking, baby talk, or climbing into the adults' bed at night, signal his need for an extra-heavy dose of parental affection and attention.

Reinforcing the child's natural instinct to make use of the "breathing space" provided by regression is the knowledge that his parents wanted a baby and the desire to make up for the loss, thereby restoring the family to its prior cohesive state. Unintentionally, one or both parents may contribute to this ambition, as the following comment by a bereaved mother suggests: "I was frightened of curtailing my children's independence, yet a part of me wanted to keep them little—at least until I could get pregnant again. We'd joke about it. At one point, I asked my daughter to keep her hair in braids for another year or two, until I straightened out . . . and both of us knew I wasn't completely kidding."

If parents recognize this tendency and, without removal of their love and protection, gently discourage it, the child will almost invariably return to the challenge of personal growth with new energy and confidence. Sometimes, however, there are more disturbing signs: "Seeing the effect of the baby's death on me gave my son a powerful weapon. Whenever I did something he didn't like, he'd blurt out, 'Okay, Mom. Tomorrow you'll have a dead kid on your hands.' I knew he was testing me, and it sent chills up my spine."

It is unfortunate that what is obvious to the parent—that the living sibling is loved every bit as much as the dead child—may appear so questionable that the youngster feels compelled to seek this kind of reassurance. Although not uncommon, the response "If I died too, you'd love me as much as you loved the baby" requires the parent's emphatic reminder that, not only is the surviving child loved, but *death is irreversible.* "I told my son," continued the mother quoted above, "that if he died he wouldn't be around to see us all mourn for him. That really seemed to penetrate. . . ."

Like the urge to regress from the threats and complexities of the near-adult world to a simpler and more sheltered stage of growth, threats of suicide are generally confined to the period directly following a loss. However, pediatrician Raymond Duff reminds parents, "It's important to separate a child's natural jealousy of a younger sibling and curiosity about death from any possibility that such a threat might be realized. Just as there must be an open dialogue in the hospital, there must be an open dialogue at home, so that the youngster receives continuing assurance from his caregivers that you don't have to die in order to be loved."

THE "REPLACEMENT CHILD" SYNDROME

Among the concerns occasionally voiced by bereaved parents is the danger of creating—either in the person of a subsequent biologic or adopted child or in one of their older surviving children—a substitute or "replacement" for the one who died. Although reports of severe juvenile pathology stemming from unresolved parental grief are rare, it is believed that many children incur lesser emotional problems related to their sense of survivorhood or competition with an idealized predecessor. Interestingly, the phenomenon is not confined to situations in which a sibling has been lost. Similar pressures to compensate for some massive void in the lives of the adults around them have been observed in the children of Holocaust victims and other survivors of disaster. Once such a child has become the repository of the family's hopes and wishes, no accomplishment, however significant, can fulfill the parents' unconsciously projected demands—for what is really desired is that which has been lost.

Some replacement children are only dimly, if at all, aware that an older brother or sister ever existed, so careful have their families been to avoid referring to the loss. They sense only that for some unexplained and disquieting reason their own achievements are never satisfactory. More extreme are those cases in which a surviving child must cope with open comparisons in which his grades, manners, or physical appearance always emerge somewhat inferior to those of the dead sibling.

Comparisons are possible even if the first child died in infancy or earlier. For example, the survivor's sex may turn out to be less satisfactory to the parent, or he or she may not bear the same resemblance to the parent, or the pregnancy/birth experience may have been less rewarding. The facts hardly matter; it is the parental attitude which poses the problem.

Dr. Elva Orlow Poznanski, a University of Michigan psychiatrist who made an intensive study of one dramatic case involving the younger of two daughters, concluded that: "Replacing a child with another allows the parents partially to deny the first child's death. The replacement child then acts as a barrier to the parental acknowledgment of death, since a real child exists who is a substitute. Thus the first stages of bereavement are prematurely arrested and the process of mourning continues indefinitely with the replacement child acting as the continuing vehicle of parental grief." [8]

In addition to bearing the full load of parental dreams and aspirations, the replacement must cope with the guilt of being, as one mother phrased it, a "privileged character": "Having the stillbirths definitely put a distance between me and my older daughter. I figured if she got here safely, why couldn't the other babies?"

In severely pathologic cases, this can lead to a subtle form of rejection in which the parents, while continuing on the surface to protect and nurture the child, actually withdraw some of their emotional investment, as though preparing for another loss. More commonly, the parental response is to treasure, but simultaneously smother and overprotect, the developing youngster.

Conscious of innumerable real and imagined dangers, the parent feels a sense of terrifying responsibility. Listen to this woman talking about her daughter's preschool years: "I felt that I had been so blessed, when finally I had the baby for whom I had prayed and waited for so long, that I had to be the perfect mother, and she the perfect child. When she wasn't, I would wonder where *I* had failed. I almost never spanked, even during the 'terrible twos.' Of course, the end result of this kind of cushioning is as bad for the child as it is for the parent. You are not equipping that growing human being to cope with life as it is. She is not going to be unequivocally accepted and loved by the world, nor will she always be excused for wrongdoing."

Clearly, parental expectations are very powerful components in shaping a child's emotional future. And even perfectly sound, enthusiastic, and caring parents are capable—for a variety of reasons belonging more to the past than the present—of loving their children "not wisely but too well." Avoiding the "replacement child" syndrome may involve delaying a subsequent pregnancy, or family counseling at a later date. Or it may simply involve parental awareness that the problem exists, and the conscious decision to allow the newcomer to function as an independent individual, free of phantoms, from infancy onward.

SOMETIMES A PROFESSIONAL CAN HELP

Pathologic family situations are often merely the exaggeration of normal conflicts. Like other problems which may be touched off or intensified by a loss in pregnancy, indications of protracted depression or other maladjustment in surviving siblings suggest that professional help should be sought. Such indications may include combinations of withdrawn or persistently regressive behavior, decline of school grades, suicidal threats, or signs of dissatisfaction with the child's sexual identity. ("You loved the baby better than me because it was a girl [or boy].")

In families with a religious orientation, consulting a trusted clergyman may be a wise first step. The clergyman, unlike the parents, is sufficiently removed from the traumatic event not to be burdened by the numbness, anger, and sense of disorientation which are normal components of bereavement. He or she is, furthermore, likely to be accustomed to probing disturbing questions with parishioners and may even have direct experience in dealing with the existential anxieties of children, having taught Sunday school, counseled other families in similar circumstances, or read extensively on the subject. Many pastoral counselors also maintain files of local psychiatric professionals to whom more complex cases can be referred.

Other parents may choose to take advantage of their local community mental health center or clinic, a crisis intervention center, or a private practitioner known for his expertise in dealing with families in distress. (Problems of this nature are almost never exclusively confined to a single family member. Rather than being the "mother's" or the "child's" problem, grief-related pathology is a family problem and should be dealt with as such.)

Regardless of who is consulted, the goals are essentially the same: to explore where each family member is, emotionally; deal honestly with both the loss and the sense of deprivation arising from it; and help parents and children express, to one another and themselves, the feelings they have previously inhibited. "The therapist, by accepting, without criticism, the anger, guilt, despair, or anxiety that the patient expresses, implicitly reassures him that such feelings, however painful, are not going to overwhelm the therapist or destroy his relationship with the patient," explains Colin Murray Parkes. "Having discovered that it is safe to express feelings the patient is now free to carry out the grief work . . . his pathological grief is transformed into 'normal grief' and follows the usual course towards resolution." [9]

It is tragic that in our culture psychosocial support is often seen as a means of last resort, a sign of serious emotional illness. Faced with a severe situational crisis such as pregnancy loss, even the most stable family may be thrown off balance for a time. Adults, like children, often regress; all need encouragement, support, and love. "The best advice for bereaved families," suggests adult/child analyst Gilbert Kliman, "is *when in doubt, consult* ' "

Books That Help Children Cope with Death

Gretchen Curtis Mills, R.N., assistant professor of nursing and continuing-education coordinator at Hampton Institute Department of Nursing in Hampton, Virginia, points out that children's literature can be an excellent source for demonstrating to youngsters that emotions can be expressed in words and that both happy and sad feelings are normal parts of living.

Ms. Mills, co-author of *Discussing Death: A Guide to Death*

Education (Palm Springs: ETC Publications, 1976), has prepared the following list of recommended titles for helping parents broach the subject.* Since the messages contained are as varied as the needs of the children they are designed to serve, it is advised that parents make a point of reading each book first themselves, to make certain it is suitable in content and reading level for their particular child.

Abbott, Sarah. *Old Dog.* New York, Coward, McCann and Geoghegen, 1972.

Alcott, Louisa. *Little Women.* New York, Macmillan and Co., 1962. (Originally published 1869.)

Anglund, J. W. *Love Is a Special Way of Feeling.* New York, Harcourt Brace Jovanovich, 1960.

———. *Morning Is a Little Child.* New York, Harcourt Brace Jovanovich, 1969.

———. *Spring Is a New Beginning.* New York, Harcourt Brace Jovanovich, 1963.

———. *What Color Is Love?* New York, Harcourt Brace Jovanovich, 1966.

Armstrong, W. H. *Sounder.* New York, Harper & Row, 1969. (Also in paperback.)

Bartoli, Jennifer. *Nonna.* Irvington-on-Hudson, N.Y., Harvey House, 1975.

Bawden, Nina. *Squib.* Philadelphia, J.B. Lippincott Co., 1971.

Berger, Terry. *I Have Feelings.* New York, Human Science Press, 1971.

Birnbaum, Abe. *Green Eyes.* Racine, Wis., Western Publishing Co., 1973. (Originally published 1953.)

Blue, Rose. *Nikki 108.* New York, Franklin Watts, 1973.

Borack, Barbara. *Someone Small.* New York, Harper & Row, 1969.

Brenner, Barbara. *Baltimore Orioles.* New York, Harper & Row, 1974.

———. *Bodies.* New York, E.P. Dutton and Co., 1973.

———. *Year in the Life of Rosie Bernard.* New York, Harper & Row, 1971.

Brooks, J. *Uncle Mike's Boy.* New York, Harper & Row, 1973.

Brown, M. W. *The Dead Bird.* Reading, Mass., Addison-Wesley Publishing Co., 1958.

Buck, P.S. *The Big Wave.* New York, John Day, 1973. (Originally published 1948.)

Carrick, Carol. *Accident.* New York, Seabury Press, 1976.

———, and Carrick, Donald. *Swamp Spring.* New York, Macmillan Co., 1969.

Cleaver, Vera, and Cleaver, Bill. *Grover.* New York. New American Library, 1975.

Coburn, J.B. *Anne and the Sand Dobbies.* New York, Seabury Press, 1964.

Cohen, Barbara. *Thank You, Jack Robinson.* New York, Lothrop, Lee & Shepard Co., 1974.

Coutant, Helen. *First Snow.* New York, Alfred A. Knopf, 1974.

* Copyright © 1979, American Journal of Nursing Company. Reprinted with permission from *American Journal of Nursing*, February, Vol. 79, No.2.

Craig, Jean. *Spring Is Like the Morning*. New York, G.P. Putnam's Sons, 1965.

De Paola, Tomie. *Nana Upstairs and Nana Downstairs*. New ed. New York, G.P. Putnam's Sons, 1973.

Dobrin, Arnold. *Scat!* New York, Scholastic Book Services, 1971.

Dunn, Phoebe. *Feelings*. Mankato, Minn., Creative Education Society, 1971.

Eunson, Dale. *The Day They Gave Babies Away*. New York, Farrar, Straus & Giroux, 1946.

Fassler, Joan. *My Grandpa Died Today*. New York, Human Science Press, 1971.

Fitzgerald, J.D. *Me and My Little Brain*. New York. Dial Press, 1971.

Greene, C.C. *Beat the Turtle Drum*. New York, Viking, 1976.

Greenfield, Eloise. *Sister*. New York, Thomas Y. Crowell, 1974.

Grollman, E. A. *Talking About Death: A Dialogue Between Parent and Child*. Boston, Beacon Press, 1976.

Harnden, Ruth. *High Pasture*. Boston, Houghton Mifflin Co., 1964 (out of print).

Harris, Audrey. *Why Did He Die?* Minneapolis, Lerner Publications Co., 1965.

Holl, Adelaide. *The Wonderful Tree*. Racine, Wis., Western Publishing Co., 1974.

Kantrowitz, Mildred. *When Violet Died*. New York, Parents' Magazine Press, 1973.

Klein, Norma. *Confessions of an Only Child*. New York, Pantheon Books, 1974.

Krauss, Ruth. *Growing Story*. New York, Harper & Row, 1947.

Lee, Virginia. *The Magic Moth*. New York, Seabury Press, 1972.

LeShan, Eda. *Learning to Say Good-By: When a Parent Dies*. New York, Macmillan Co., 1976.

McNulty, Faith. *Woodchuck*. New York, Harper & Row, 1974.

Miles, Miska. *Annie and the Old One*. Boston, Little, Brown and Company, 1971.

Molloy, A. S. *The Girl from Two Miles High*. New York, Hastings House Publishers, 1967.

Orgell, Doris. *Mulberry Music*. New York, Harper & Row, 1971.

Parker, B. M. *The Wonders of the Seasons*. Racine, Wis., Western Publishing Co., 1974.

Pringle, Laurence. *Death Is Natural*. New York. Scholastic Book Services, 1977.

Rock, Gail. *The House Without a Christmas Tree*. New York, Alfred A. Knopf, 1974.

———. *The Thanksgiving Treasure*. New York, Alfred A. Knopf, 1974.

Shecter, Ben. *Someplace Else*. New York, Harper & Row, 1971.

Shotwell, L. R. *Adam Bookout*. New York, Viking Press, 1967.

Simon, Norma. *How Do I Feel?* Chicago, Albert Whitman and Co., 1970.

Smith, D. B. *A Taste of Blackberries*. New York, Thomas Y. Crowell, 1973. (Paperback 1976.)

Stein, S. B. *About Dying: An Open Book for Parents and Children Together*. New York, Walker and Co., 1974.

Tresselt, Alvin. *The Dead Tree*. New York. Parents' Magazine Press, 1972.

Viorst, Judith. *The Tenth Good Thing About Barney*. New York, Atheneum Publishers, 1971.

Warburg, S. S. *Growing Time*. Boston, Houghton Mifflin Co., 1969.

White, E. B. *Charlotte's Web*. New York, Harper & Row, 1952.

Wiggin, K. D. *The Birds' Christmas Carol*. Boston, Houghton Mifflin Co., 1941.

Zim, H. S., and Bleeker, Sonia. *Life and Death*. New York, William Morrow and Co., 1970.

Zolotow, Charlotte. *My Grandson Lew*. New York, Harper & Row, 1974.

6
Looking Ahead

THREE MONTHS, six months, a year or two? While the optimal timing of a new conception following unsuccessful pregnancy is a widely discussed topic among health professionals, many parents agonize over whether to try again at all. As one father expressed it: "Sure, we want to have a child. But I am terrified of letting my wife go through another pregnancy. That's the only way we can relate to it now, as something to be "gotten through." The excitement, the upbeat mood that characterized our first effort is gone."

Like the victim of a serious auto accident who finds a hundred excuses for not getting behind the wheel again, the mother may tell herself that she wants to become pregnant . . . only not this month. "It's been two years since my miscarriage," said one woman at a meeting of a parents' group, "and I keep thinking, next month will be the right time. Lately, I've begun to wonder if there ever will be a 'right' time." Interjected another: "Originally I was hesitant to become pregnant because I wasn't certain I could handle the responsibility of being a mother. Now that I believe it's what I want, I'm hesitant because I know the dangers."

Or the father may be the one to resist. "My husband didn't seem to grieve at all, at first," commented the mother of a stillborn. "But now that I've accepted it and feel ready to plan another child, he's backing off. He thinks we need more time. The trouble is, I'm thirty-four, so there isn't a whole lot of time left." (This is a fairly common reaction. Because denial inhibits real acceptance and integration of the loss, a woman may emerge from a long siege of depression considerably comforted, only to find her formerly stoical mate full of new doubts and anxieties.)

Other parents are anxious to get started. Marion Cohen remembers responding angrily to the counselors who suggested that she wait longer than the basic postpartum recovery period: "Grief process, schmief process, I thought. What's wrong with having another teeny little baby growing in my belly while I'm mourning this one? I might as well be *happy* while I'm going through the grief process!"

Medical conditions and emotional responses to the crisis of bereavement are so variable that it is impossible to come up with a prescription which will suit every family. While a few months of physical recuperation following perinatal death are always recommended—possibly longer, if there has been an additional complication such as pelvic infection—in most instances the body heals quickly.

Emotional scars are another matter. Here, professional opinion is more divided. A 1970 study by Dr. John R. Wolff and colleagues at the Presbyterian-St. Luke's Hospital in Chicago found that, of forty women who lost a baby at or shortly after birth, the resolution in 50 percent of the cases lay in becoming pregnant again. Eighty percent of these pregnancies were planned immediately after the baby's death. "This," reported the researchers, "could be viewed as satisfying a maternal need and possibly playing a significant role in maintaining psychic equilibrium." [1]

On the other hand, in the remaining 50 percent of cases other pathways of resolution were chosen, including returning to or beginning employment, going to school, or intensifying family and household activities. A large number of women were adamant about not having another child, and half of those resorted to sterilization during the three-year followup. Although hospital procedures, patient accommodations, and the attitudes of staff following the loss played a role in the mothers' comfort, these did not appear to affect their decision-making with respect to a subsequent pregnancy. Concluded Wolff et al.: "Our data indicated that the individual woman may take one direction or the other (pregnancy or nonpregnancy) and function equally well in either state." [2]

Other studies have taken a more definite stance in favor of delay. In one 1978 report by Jane Rowe, M.D., and colleagues at the University of California, San Francisco, six out of twenty-six mothers interviewed by telephone ten to twenty-two months after perinatal death were judged to have experienced a morbid or prolonged grief reaction. "These six mothers," observed the researchers, "did not differ from the twenty mothers who showed no evidence of a prolonged grief reaction in age, economic class, cause of infant death, age of the infant at the time of death, the presence of a child in the home, or the interval between the infant's death and the interview. The only factor we found associated with a morbid grief reaction was the presence of a new infant in the home, closely following the death of the index child, i.e., mothers who had either a surviving twin or who became pregnant less than five months after the death were significantly more likely to show signs of prolonged, morbid grief response at the time of the interview than were those who had no subsequent pregnancy or one more than six months later." [3]

In talking with the investigators, mothers who were judged to have a morbid reaction commonly made such statements as: "I can't get close to my new baby. I find I'm short-tempered. I'm building up a little wall in case anything happens to him." In view of the possibility that early subsequent pregnancy may interfere with normal grieving, Rowe et al. caution that: "Both the increased risks to the next infant and the potential psychological risks to the parents should temper physicians' enthusiasm for encouraging families to 'go right ahead and have another baby.' " [4]

Complicating the decision, however, may be the question of maternal age. Dr. Zena Stein, director of New York State's Epidemiology of Mental Retardation Research Unit at Columbia University, points out: "Today, many women are delaying their first pregnancy until their mid-thirties. They don't have the biological luxury of waiting nine months to a year after a loss before trying again. The physiologic risks associated with an increased delay may ultimately outweigh the psychological benefits."

Rather than wait for a specified time, pediatrician Raymond Duff suggests that "parents should let their own feelings with regard to the state of their recovery guide them. In particular: Can they put the loss behind them and make a fresh start?" In fact, because partners often disagree and some vacillation is not the exception but the rule, the final decision is often left to chance. Commented a smiling woman in her eighth month of pregnancy, "My husband's initial response was not to want another baby, but I really wanted a second child, so we agreed to try again at some unspecified time. As it turned out, despite our decision to wait we found ourselves being careless about birth control. I suppose that secretly we both were hoping that Fate would step in. . . ."

THE PRE-PREGNANCY LETDOWN

The suitcase is waiting, for some time next year.
The suitcase is waiting, with Carter's undershirts
   size 3 months and birth announcements
   and nightgowns that button down the front.
Yesterday I noticed that one latch had come undone
   and the suitcase had partially opened up
   and the nightgowns were spilling out.
The suitcase is waiting, but not very patiently.
       —*Marion Cohen,*
       FROM "DOES TIME HEAL ALL WOUNDS?"

Having decided that they are emotionally ready to go ahead with another pregnancy, the couple refrain from birth control measures and wait tensely—often, no more than a few menstrual cycles. However, other bereaved parents find, to their distress, that this anxious period of "cliffhanging" lasts far longer than anticipated.

A young woman we'll call Alice—already the mother of a five-year-old daughter—describes her experience: "I had what is known as a 'missed abortion,' in that I miscarried somewhere between the seventh and the tenth week, and found out about it two months later. This was followed by a D&C [dilatation and curettage, or scraping of the uterine lining, under anesthesia, to remove the contents]. A few months later, we tried to get me pregnant again, and found that we couldn't. Not having had any problems with my first pregnancy, I was completely unprepared for the three-year ordeal that followed.

"The first gynecologist I consulted put me on Clomid [clomiphene citrate, a synthetic agent used primarily to promote ovulation] without doing a really comprehensive workup. After six months, when I still hadn't ovulated, he finally got around to ordering a hysterosalpingogram [an X-ray examination of the uterine cavity and fallopian tubes by means of radio-opaque dye injected through the cervix], which showed that I had uterine adhesions, probably stemming from the D&C. This required additional surgery; still, no conception. I switched gynecologists, and had a more thorough workup, which showed that I had an underactive thyroid as well as more adhesions—apparently, the surgery hadn't been able to eradicate them completely. This time, I was placed on thyroid medication, and with very high hopes of success we waited again.

"After three months, I felt I'd had my fill of specialists and decided to consult the chiropractor recommended by a friend. But although his diet/vitamin regimen made me feel a whole lot healthier, after another six months I *still* wasn't ovulating. Close to giving up, my husband and I finally did what we ought to have considered all along—consulted an infertility specialist. More thyroid medication, followed by another trial of Clomid. . . . This time, I began ovulating, but my temperature chart continued to show abnormal fluctuations. Again, months went by, and again we became discouraged. I sensed myself getting older. My husband and I argued about whether to change course and try to adopt a baby. Both of us were exhausted by the years of tests, by the record-keeping and the intrusion into our sex life.

"Finally, I told the infertility specialist that I wanted to go back into the hospital for surgery on the remaining adhesions. No more Clomid. On the Monday I was scheduled for surgery, my doctor received a telephone call from the hospital lab. The blood tests I'd had on admission indicated that I was pregnant! He warned me that the results were probably false. Still, the D&C was postponed until further tests could be done. These, too, were positive, and nine months later our son was born."

Although longer and more frustrating than most, Alice's experience was hardly unique. Such a high percentage of temporarily infertile couples conceive after having reached an important decision regarding their childlessness—for example, consulting a new physician, hospital admission for testing, the decision to adopt—that several authors have suggested a link between relief of stress and the removal of some chemical barrier to fertility.

This in no way implies that anxiety always correlates with delays in conception, or that nothing more is required of the would-be parents than to "go home and relax." (Many extremely tense and anxious, as well as neurotic and psychotic, women do not encounter difficulties in becoming pregnant.) It simply indicates that the kind of stress-related hormonal changes which have been observed in conjunction with other somatic conditions may also be a factor in the fertility problems that sometimes follow a loss in pregnancy.

> Anything, I'll do anything—
> Temperature charts, Tes-Tape, litmus paper,
> Vitamin A, Vitamin E, zinc, manganese,
> Abstinence to maximize sperm count,
> Lying on my back with a pillow under my behind
>   and my legs up like a beetle.
> Anything, I'll do anything—
> But please—please—don't ask me just to relax.
> —*Marion Cohen,*
> "TRYING-TO-CONCEIVE POEM #4"

Inasmuch as the recommendation to relax is nearly useless in itself, a better approach might be for the caregiver to suggest a number of general measures aimed at taking some of the pressure off the couple and promoting the mother's physical health and self-esteem. Has she been eating sensibly and receiving plenty of rest and exercise? (Fatigue is a depressant from every standpoint imaginable.) If much of her time is still spent at home, brooding over the loss, has she considered returning to school or work, increasing her participation in community volunteer activities, or joining a parent support group? Do the couple go out regularly, to dinner, movies, or the theater? Do they take a few days off now and then for a weekend at a beach or ski resort, to go camping, to play tennis or golf? If family conflicts are clearly contributing to the general tension, would a course of supportive psychotherapy be a logical next step?

Finally, rather than brushing aside the mother's concerns about her reproductive capacity, the physician can say something like: "You are obviously tense about this, and with good reason. This is a difficult time for you and your family. However, I can assure you that *it is highly unlikely that your anxiety in itself will prevent a pregnancy.* If every woman who was afraid of or conflicted about bearing a child would be unable to conceive on that account alone, the producers of birth control devices would go out of business, and we know this is not the case."

PREGNANT AGAIN

"The oddest thing," said Alice at the close of her story, "was that we weren't even exhilarated when they told us I was pregnant. For three years, Jim and I had talked about nothing except this baby. We had our own fantasy: the telephone would ring and a voice from the lab would say: 'Congratulations, you are going to be a mother.' Instead, there I was in the hospital, shot through with medication in preparation for my third D&C. It seemed all wrong. Even my gynecologist believed that the test results were probably mistaken! Of course, I wanted the baby. But I was scared that I might abort, and scared of the unknown effects of all the drugs I had been given if I *didn't*."

Neither Alice's sense of anticlimax, nor her fears with respect to the conception which, happily, produced a healthy eight-pound baby boy, were in any degree unusual. Fact rarely matches fantasy. And there is a desperate quality about these hard-won pregnancies, a sense of "lost innocence," which many couples find deeply troubling.

"My first pregnancy seemed so effortless," reminisced a woman who was drawing close to her second due date. "Decorating the nursery, buying little blankets and T-shirts and comparing notes with other mothers-to-be . . . that's what I thought having a baby was all about. That just isn't me any more."

"Be optimistic, think only positive thoughts, is all I hear," added another. "The fact is, what's really on my mind is: What if I lose this one, too?" Other mothers have described the feeling as having a "cloud" hovering over the new pregnancy, especially until they passed the point at which death had formerly occurred.

> L'il Fetus, I apologize
> For the cold winds in my womb.
> What happened here
> Must have left a chill,
> A few cold patches among the warm.
> L'il Fetus, I apologize
> That your house is haunted.
> L'il Fetus, I apologize
> But it's the only house I have.
> —*Marion Cohen,*
> FROM "FOURTH PREGNANCY"

Even when (as is most often the case) the first loss has been identified as a random occurrence, worries persist. "I was terrified during the entire pregnancy," recalled one mother as she nursed her daughter during a lull in our conversation. "Whenever the baby didn't move, or moved too much, I got upset. If I gained very little weight one month or developed a cold, I would wonder for weeks afterward what effect this was having on the baby."

Some women develop insomnia. Others become intensely conscious of the foods they eat, going to great lengths to arm themselves nutritionally against particular problems. Cigarettes and alcohol are sworn off. "No more fooling around," summed up one expectant mother, between bites of spinach salad. "This time, I'm giving it my best shot."

Even women who ordinarily are not superstitious become conscious of a strong desire not to "tempt Fate." This is really another variant of the "magical thinking" response described in Chapter 3 (see "Bargaining," p. 61). Unconsciously, the expectant mother has made a connection between the optimistic mood of her prior pregnancy and its tragic outcome. As a consequence, she now tries to gain a measure of control over things by proceeding with the utmost caution—not sharing the news with friends or relatives, perhaps even postponing an appointment with the gynecologist—in the hope that, by ignoring the pregnancy, she can magically influence its outcome.

"The first time I was pregnant," Connie Purcell recalls, "Mike and I practically shouted the news from the rooftops. Our second pregnancy seemed much more fragile. We waited several weeks before telling our parents, our good friends didn't know until the sixth or seventh month, and others found out only when they received the birth announcement." (The myth that human pregnancy may evoke divine jealousy is common to many cultures. The mysteries of childbirth, with its delicate balance of life and death, have awed and inspired and filled humanity with fear since the dawn of creation. Among certain primitive peoples, it is the custom for a pregnant woman to wear a charm or amulet, to ward off the wrath of any deity who may be jealous of her accomplishment.)

Afraid of placing too great an emotional investment in the unborn child, the couple may consciously avoid referring to the pregnancy even among themselves. "We tried not to think about the baby as 'he' or 'she' or make any concrete plans for its arrival," commented a relieved father after a difficult but successful second pregnancy. "Really, we were just holding our breaths."

As the critical months pass, hopes are slowly reborn. Most anxious of all are the small minority of women who, for reasons that are obvious or only poorly understood, have experienced recurrent losses. Nurse-clinician and author Sheila Garvey, a juvenile diabetic who by age thirty-three had seen eight pregnancies end tragically, describes her ninth:

"I had suffered so many disappointments that I began to set goals for myself. The moment of quickening was very important, because that was when I first allowed myself to hope. Hearing the fetal heartbeat was another milestone; reaching the age of viability yet another. During the final weeks of my last pregnancy, I was warned by my obstetrician that the baby was likely to be stillborn because of increasingly severe complications of my diabetes. Yet somehow I never completely lost faith. I cannot explain it intellectually, but there was something in me that knew that on this, my final try, we were going to make it." (And Sheila did. At this writing, her daughter, Kerry Beth, is twelve years old.)

Because the birth of a new infant is really another milestone in the painful process of saying good-bye to the one who died, it may take some time before the parents allow themselves to relax and accept the reassertion of life. Nurses Pauline M. Seitz and Louise H. Warrick, who intensively studied the responses of formerly bereaved mothers to their healthy newborns, report that: "The mourning of the mother's previous loss may be observed to be very intense during the first few days postpartum with her new baby. The mother compares the babies, her pregnancies, and childbirth experiences. She should be encouraged to talk about the differences and to reinforce the healthy aspects and signs of viability in her new baby." [5]

If the mother is wary of immediate contact with her new infant, her feelings should be respected, say Seitz and Warrick. Slowly, as she becomes comfortable with the child's viability, she will begin to see the baby as a person in his or her own right, let down her guard, and begin to love.

"Nobody could believe how tense I was," reported a woman whose previous child had been stillborn. "For at least a week after we brought our baby home from the hospital, I would stay up twenty-four hours, until there were big, black circles under my eyes, watching him."

It is not uncommon for either or both parents to worry that the doctors and nurses are incompetent, or untrustworthy, and the baby's condition is not really as good as it appears; or that Fate, suddenly so benevolent, will trick them and take away their baby just as they are allowing themselves to grow attached to him or her. Yet despite these initial fears, after the first few weeks most couples find their qualms fading—replaced by an intense joy and absorption in the challenge of new parenthood.

As in any postpartum period, however, there are still adjustments to be made. First-time parents, in particular, usually find their previous ideas of what living with a new baby will be like rarely substantiated by fact. That *this* particular infant—quite oblivious to the difficult emotional journey undertaken by his parents on his behalf—should occasionally cry, spit up, develop diaper rash, and generally make a nuisance of himself like any other normal baby, seems an unfair burden!

There are also special concerns directly related to the pregnancy history. Many couples worry about spoiling the new baby by giving it twice the love and attention it deserves (impossible) and half the discipline (distinctly possible, and to be avoided). Others fear that, if the infant is of the same gender as the child who died, there will be some confusion of identities; or, if not of the same gender, that this baby will ultimately be less gratifying to them on that account.

Sometimes, too, there is a peculiar emotional letdown which comes when the mother realizes her long struggle to produce a healthy child is over. "Becoming a parent had been the goal of my life for so long," explained one thirty-eight-year-old career-woman-turned-homemaker, "that I found it difficult to accept that I'd reached my destination when I finally got there. Now there are days when I feel discontented, when I look for a new focus, when I say to myself: 'Okay, now what do I do for an encore?' "

The woman quoted above is the adoptive mother of a bright and bubbly two-year-old girl. Numerous infertility workups, followed by a mid-trimester spontaneous abortion, convinced her and her husband that adopting a baby was the right road for them. "During my pregnancy," she recalls, "I was so happy finally to be expecting that the baby didn't seem very real to me. Afterward, when I had time to evaluate it, I realized that being pregnant was really much less important to me than being a mother. You might say that the focus gradually shifted from wanting to be pregnant, for pregnancy's sake, to wanting a *child*, for the child's sake."

Parenting a child, whether biologic or adoptive, is such a dynamic, all-engrossing task that many couples worry that they will forget the past altogether. Can we, they wonder, go on as any other happy family, without being unfaithful to our memories? Connie Purcell comments: "Even with the incredibly sweet and bright six-month-old daughter we have, there are times when we both stop and wonder: What would he have been like, our son? Who would he have been? The pain ebbs, and there are new sources of happiness. But whenever we think about our first pregnancy, there is a sense of loss."

7
Searching for Answers

I pestered my doctors with questions, because it seemed so important to understand what had happened from a medical point of view. It's difficult enough to deal with a tragedy if you know what's going on; dealing with a tragedy you *don't* understand is much harder.

"WHY, DOCTOR?" THE question is asked by every bereaved parent, not once but fifty or a hundred times. What went wrong? *Whose fault was it?*

Chances are that the fault, if it can be called that, lay not with the parents or medical staff but with any one (or more) of the hundreds of genetic, metabolic, or environmental factors which may threaten fetal development. Comments Silvio Aladjem, M.D., chairman of obstetrics and gynecology at the Loyola University Stritch School of Medicine in Chicago: "Nature is cruel; if allowed to proceed without medical aid, childbearing is accompanied by a high fetal mortality and morbidity as well as a level of maternal mortality and morbidity unacceptable in the twentieth century." [1]

While certain maternal-fetal hazards have been enormously reduced by advances in diagnostic testing and therapeutic refinements, others—notably, those related to contamination of our air, soil, and water by an expanding galaxy of toxic industrial wastes and other chemical pollutants—are on the increase. How to deal with these, as well as ensure that the up-to-date technologies now becoming avail-

127

able are taken advantage of by pregnant women regardless of age, race, or socioeconomic status, will constitute the two greatest challenges of twenty-first-century obstetrics.

The following chapter is designed for couples seeking more specific factual information about the causes of unsuccessful pregnancy. Obviously, space limitations prevent our listing every factor involved, and many areas of considerable significance (e.g., infection) are touched upon only briefly. Readers desiring more detailed information may wish to consult the bibliography located on p. 161. Other literature can be obtained through county medical societies, the March of Dimes Birth Defects Foundation, local parent support groups, medical and nursing school bookstores, the public library, and your own physician.

Instructions to the Fetus *

Choose a young, healthy mother of good socioeconomic status who is over 64 inches tall, slender, Rh positive, and has a regular menstrual cycle.

She must not smoke, take drugs, or seek medication. Her family background must be genetically impeccable, and she must seek good antenatal care and a safe place in which to deliver.

So order your own environment and request that you are not born either preterm or postterm. Let not your membranes rupture early, and, above all, enter the world head first with the minimum delay once the journey has started. Having arrived, breathe quickly before they cut your cord, and then ask to be directed to the intensive care unit!

By this you have the best chance to survive the risks of your prenatal life.

OBSTETRICAL RISKS

Preclinical Pregnancies

Although verification is impossible, it is suspected that a large number of embryonic losses occur during the first four weeks of gestation—even before the woman realizes that she is pregnant. Without

* From Silvio Aladjem. *Risks in the Practice of Modern Obstetrics*, 2nd ed. (St. Louis: The C. V. Mosby Company, 1975), p. 1.

clinical proof that conception has occurred, couples who repeatedly experience such unrecognized fetal losses may be thought to be infertile. Dr. Joe Leigh Simpson, chief of the Section on Human Genetics at Northwestern University Medical School in Chicago, points out that some physicians loosely apply the term "infertility" to any patient who has been unable to complete a pregnancy successfully, even if the cause is not infertility *per se* but repetitive spontaneous abortions.

Very early losses may result from either genetic or nongenetic causes. Gross chromosomal abnormalities affecting the preimplantation and early implantation stages of life are believed to be extremely common. Investigations of lower animals (rats, wild rabbits, pigs) suggest that as many as 40 percent of fertilized eggs fail to come to delivery, and that of these losses about 10 percent occur in the fallopian tube and nearly 85 percent at or near the time of implantation. In most instances, the defective egg or sperm cell appears to be a chance abnormality. The couple are perfectly capable of producing normal cells, and future pregnancies are carried to term without incident.

The logical conclusion—that there exists in all species a natural protective mechanism against the development of abnormal offspring—has given rise to the unfortunate tendency of caregivers to dismiss early spontaneous abortions as "for the best" when counseling bereaved parents. Obviously, the birth of a living but severely malformed or retarded child represents an agony to the parents and a great cost to society. However, it is generally difficult for couples (especially if there have been repetitive abortions) to regard the matter in such a cold light.

What *is* abundantly clear is that we really know very little about the causes and implications of these early embryonic losses. Notes epidemiologist Zena Stein: "The fact that it frequently requires repeated, well-timed exposures for an apparently fertile woman to become pregnant would seem to suggest that this early period holds inherent dangers to the embryo, of which, at the present time, we are only dimly aware."

Ectopic Pregnancies

An ectopic pregnancy is any gestation which implants outside the uterine cavity. The majority of ectopic pregnancies occur in the fallopian tube—the hollow structure which leads the fertilized egg to the uterus.

A woman's fallopian tubes may be narrow due to some developmental defect, or they may have been distorted or scarred by previous episodes of pelvic inflammation and infection. Regardless of the history, in roughly 1 percent of pregnancies the ovum fails to reach the uterus and, instead, lodges in the wall of the fallopian tube. At some point, usually within the first twelve weeks, the growing egg either erodes and ruptures the wall of the tube or aborts through its open end. The products of conception, often accompanied by large quantities of blood, flow into the abdominal cavity, and the woman experiences sudden severe pain. This may be accompanied by vaginal spotting and, if bleeding is extensive, symptoms of shock.

Surgical removal of the tube (or, in selected cases, only the affected portion) and blood transfusion to offset the effects of hemorrhage are critical, as this is a life-threatening situation. Rarely, survival of the embryo may occur—incidents are occasionally reported in which the placenta, after growing through the tubal wall, has implanted on other structures and obtained enough blood supply to allow the fetus to develop to full term in the peritoneal cavity (abdominal pregnancy).

Following an ectopic pregnancy, a woman's chances of never becoming pregnant again are in the 30 percent range, with an additional third of patients experiencing a repeat ectopic. Because of this rather poor prognosis, considerable effort has been directed toward preserving fertility in women who have already lost one tube and then experience a second ectopic in the remaining tube. A procedure now exists whereby only the portion of the tube containing the pregnancy is removed, so that the severed ends may be sewn back together under a microscope after the inflammation has subsided. Although not yet in widespread use, this technique offers women who have experienced successive ectopics new hope of achieving a successful pregnancy.

Molar Pregnancies

Molar pregnancy is a rare event (about one in 2,000 pregnancies in the United States) with an estimated risk of recurrence of about 2 percent. The cause of the abnormality is unknown, although immunologic and nutritional deficiencies may play a role.

At first, pregnancy may appear to be proceeding normally; however, there is no fetus present. Instead, the placenta develops into an abnormal mass of grapelike fluid-filled sacs, called vesicles. Bleeding and severe episodes of vomiting may be early danger signals. If the woman does not abort spontaneously in the first trimester, this placental tumor enlarges rapidly and severe hemorrhage may follow.

Treatment consists of evacuating the uterus by whichever means is most appropriate to the size of the tumor at the time of diagnosis. Evacuation must be carried out with great care to avoid injuring the uterine wall. Tissue samples are then sent for pathologic examination, since there is a risk that choriocarcinoma—a cancerous growth of the abnormal placenta—may develop. Although this is a rare complication, without therapy it can be deadly. Therefore, any woman who has had a molar pregnancy owes herself the protection of frequent gynecologic visits and careful followup.

Early Fetal Loss

The first trimester of pregnancy (up to twelve weeks gestation) is the time of greatest vulnerability for the fetus. Seventy-five percent of clinically recognized spontaneous abortions, or "miscarriages," take place during this period—the remainder occurring from the thirteenth week until the age of viability, after which they are officially considered perinatal deaths.

It is estimated that at least 20 percent of pregnant women will have symptoms of threatened abortion, bleeding and occasionally cramping, at some point during the first months of pregnancy. Although many physicians advise curtailment of physical activity when bleeding occurs, and some even advocate bed rest, such precautionary measures are largely ineffective at this early stage. (Bed rest may be beneficial in later pregnancy, if there is an expectation of premature labor.) The bleeding will either taper off of its own accord or progress to "inevitable" abortion, regardless of what is or is not done to prevent it. Administration of large doses of progesterone—once advocated as a treatment for threatened abortion—has been discredited on the grounds that such therapy, by inhibiting the uterine contractions which expel the products of conception, may result in either a "missed" abortion or increased risk of hormone-related abnormalities if the fetus is liveborn.

When abortion does follow, as it does in about 50 percent of cases, the most common cause is a genetic abnormality in the fetus.

In at least half of all miscarriages, the correct human complement of forty-six chromosomes (twenty-two paired autosomes, identified by numbers 1 through 22, plus one pair of sex chromosomes) have been reshuffled, duplicated, or lost in a way which is generally incompatible with life. Sometimes the abnormality is numerical, involving the addition or loss of one or more chromosomes. At other times, a structural defect may result in the "translocation" of a chromosome or chromosome fragment from one chromosome pair to another. Incidence is greatest among early losses, declining to about 10 to 20 percent by the second trimester. Among stillborn infants, the incidence of chromosomal anomalies is only around 5 percent.

Although the majority of defects are believed to result from random mistakes of genetic arrangement, some, such as Down's syndrome, can be familial in origin. Since the clinical picture of an inherited disorder may mimic that of one which is random, comprehensive genetic studies—involving establishment of a family genetic history or "pedigree" and graphic representation of the fetal chromosome arrangement by a process known as karyotyping—may be required to make the distinction. (See "Why Genetic Testing," p. 139.)

It is well known that random errors in the maturation of egg cells prior to fertilization are more common in women nearing the end of their reproductive lives. Since a lifetime supply of eggs is present in the female body at birth, these may simply become "overripe" as a woman matures. In addition, the higher incidence of hormonal imbalance and irregular menses among older obstetrical patients suggest that delays in the timing of ovulation and fertilization of the egg may contribute to its eventual deterioration and expulsion.

Regardless of the cause, treatment of spontaneous abortion depends upon the mother's condition on hospital admission and her physician's assessment of the degree of uterine evacuation. Although no surgical treatment is ordinarily required when the products of conception have been completely expelled, an incomplete abortion must be completed by a D&C (sometimes known as D&E, or dilatation and evacuation) as a precaution against infection and further bleeding. Occasionally, a woman's symptoms may be so mild that death is not detected until several weeks or months afterward. Such pregnancy loss is called a "missed" abortion and is treated in the same manner as an incomplete abortion—by mechanical evacuation of the uterine contents under anesthesia.

Although a single miscarriage is believed to involve only a very minimal risk of recurrence beyond that encountered in a first pregnancy, the expelled products of conception should be saved for laboratory examination whenever possible. (In very early pregnancy, embryonic tissue is often passed without detection in clotted blood.) Since spontaneous abortion is the most common form of pregnancy loss, affecting hundreds of thousands of U.S. couples annually, the amount of scientific data which can be acquired by careful investigation of even a small percentage of these isolated incidents is formidable.

Furthermore, if we view reproductive casualty as a continuous spectrum—with birth defects at one end and early fetal losses at the other—it follows that information concerning the frequency of genetic abnormalities and other characteristics of the aborted embryo has definite implications for perinatal and infant health, as well. By piecing such information together, teams of physicians and epidemiologists have already begun to find answers, or at least suggestions, for the origin of many fetal deaths previously dismissed as "of unknown cause." The recent identification of alcohol intake and cigarette smoking as distinct contributors to unsuccessful pregnancy are two examples of scientific breakthroughs resulting from this kind of detective work.

The toxic effects of certain industrial pollutants on maternal *and paternal* reproductive capacity and obstetrical outcome are also receiving widespread attention. Over 40 percent of the U.S. workforce is currently female. Tens of thousands of women are employed in high-risk industries, involving exposure to toxic dusts, chemicals, and ionizing radiation. In addition, the highly publicized rash of pregnancy losses and birth defects at New York State's Love Canal and other chemically contaminated sites offers grim evidence that teratogenic and mutagenic compounds may be found in the water a woman drinks while pregnant, in the air she breathes, or in the soil outside her front door.

Environmental Pollutants *	Reproductive Outcomes Associated with Parental Exposure *
Macroenvironmental:	
Heavy metals: mercury, lead, cadmium, nickel	Altered fertility pattern
Chlorinated dibenzo-p-	Spontaneous abortion

* From Lawrence D. Longo, "Environmental Pollution and Pregnancy: Risks and Uncertainties for the Fetus and Infant," *American Journal of Obstetrics and Gynecology* 137: 2 (May 15, 1980), p. 163.

Environmental Pollutants	Reproductive Outcomes Associated with Parental Exposure †
dioxins: TCDD	
Polychlorinated and polybrominated biphenyls: PCB, PBB	Chromosomal abnormalities
Organochlorine pesticides	Nonchromosomal congenital defects
Polycyclic aromatic hydrocarbons	Altered sex ratio
Air pollutants: carbon monoxide, ozone	Late fetal death Neonatal death
Radiation	Low birthweight
Microenvironmental (social environmental):	Developmental disabilities Behavioral disorders
Tobacco smoke: carbon monoxide, nicotine, polycyclic aromatic hydrocarbons	Childhood malignancies Childhood death
Alcohol	
Drugs: opiates, barbiturates, anesthetics, sex steroids	
Food additives	

† Modified from Sullivan, F. M., and Barlow, S. M.: Congenital malformations and other reproductive hazards from environmental chemicals, Proc. R. Soc. Lond. (Biol.) 205:91, 1979.

Recurrent Spontaneous Abortion

Another area of scientific concern relates to those rare but unfortunate women who experience repetitive spontaneous abortions, usually in the second trimester. The psychological consequences of such a string of reproductive casualties can be so devastating that for many years physicians overstressed the psychogenic aspects of the problem. In fact, while a course of supportive psychotherapy may prove valuable, the patient's anxiety is far more likely to be the *effect*, rather than the *cause*, of her condition.

A thorough medical workup and genetic studies can rule out the presence of most chronic maternal disease, infection, hormonal imbalance, uterine structural defect, or detectable chromosomal anomalies. Often, no specific treatable abnormality is found. Even after many disappointments, however, the couple can be reassured that the situation is far from hopeless. Whereas twenty years ago a woman who had experienced three or more consecutive losses might be labeled a "habitual aborter" and told that her chances of eventual success were as low as 10 percent, recent studies have shown success rates to be in the neighborhood of 70 or 80 percent—only slightly below those in the general population.

Emotional support from the woman's family and a good rapport with her physician can ease tensions and reduce the expectation of failure which may or may not be a contributing factor in poor outcome. Administration of progestins, vitamin supplements, or thyroid medication is *not* indicated unless a deficiency has been shown to exist in one of these areas.

Why do certain women find it so difficult to carry a pregnancy up to the age of viability? The question, which has baffled physicians for years, is made all the more elusive by the fact that a number of treatable conditions—including benign tumors, uterine structural abnormalities, and infection with organisms of the mycoplasma group—appear to be significant factors in some women but not in others. Currently, research is centering on the possibilities of biochemical disturbances in the intrauterine environment and rejection of the fetus by the mother's immune system.

It has been known for some time that unlike first-trimester losses, later spontaneous abortions tend to involve genetically normal fetuses. In the 1970s, a study by geneticists at Columbia University in New York indicated a link between repetitive late fetal losses and a history of conception problems, on the one hand, and prior premature delivery of a low-birthweight infant, on the other. In other words, women who exhibited infertility problems, or at least (unplanned) wide intervals between pregnancies, would often go on to either abort spontaneously in mid-pregnancy or deliver before gestation was complete. In the absence of abnormalities in the fetus, the investigators surmised that some maternal condition (such as a hormone insufficiency) or a maternal-fetal blood group incompatibility might be responsible for premature onset of labor. Since the "repeaters" also showed a strong tendency to initiate labor at roughly the same point in pregnancy each time, it was further suggested that there might be two separate pathological mechanisms at work: one operating around the time of conception and accounting for the infertility problems and early losses, the other becoming more prominent as gestation progressed. Other studies have pointed to a particular immunologic difficulty—the absence in maternal blood of an antibody known as "blocking factor," which ordinarily protects the fetus from rejection by the mother's body. Should this prove to be the case, it eventually may be possible to anticipate the problem and administer blocking factor to expectant women lacking it.

Uterine Abnormalities

For the fertilized egg to develop normally, it requires (1) a secure implantation site or foothold in the uterine wall, (2) adequate nourishment from the placental blood supply, and (3) ample room for growth within the uterine cavity. If any of these is lacking, fetal deterioration and/or premature expulsion from the uterus is likely to follow.

The mechanisms by which structural abnormalities of the uterine tract interfere with these requisites for fetal survival are often unclear. It is known, however, that cervical incompetence, Asherman's syndrome, Müllerian abnormalities, and benign tumors of the uterus can predispose certain woman to pregnancy loss, generally in the second or early third trimester.

Cervical Incompetence. Unlike other forms of miscarriage, which are often marked by painful cramping like that of term labor, pregnancy loss associated with cervical incompetence is generally painless. Forced open by the downward pressure of the growing fetus, the weakened cervix simply dilates and allows its contents to pass through. Various explanations have been offered, most involving prior trauma to cervical tissues from a difficult vaginal birth, D&C, conization, or cauterization procedures. Unfortunately, diagnosis usually *follows* at least one suspiciously painless mid-pregnancy loss. Once confirmed, various steps can be taken to correct the abnormality, the most reliable involving encircling the cervical opening with a resilient cloth suture, which reinforces the tissues until the actual start of labor (at which time the sutures must be cut, or cesarean section performed, to avoid rupturing the uterus). There are many variations of surgical technique—the Shirodkar-Barter and McDonald being the most popular—claiming success rates up to 80 percent.

Asherman's Syndrome. Asherman's syndrome is characterized by the presence of adhesions (scars) which obstruct the uterine wall and are believed to hinder implantation of the fertilized egg. These may result from too-aggressive curettage or other intrauterine surgery, or from pelvic infection. Diagnosis is by hysterosalpingogram (see p. 120). Although the actual influence of uterine adhesions on pregnancy outcome is uncertain, lysis or cutting away of the scar tissue has been associated with improved survival figures.

Müllerian Abnormalities. It is estimated that between 2 and 3 percent of women have congenital abnormalities of uterine structure related to the failure of two embryonic tubes, known as the Müllerian ducts, to fuse together during gestation. Examples are unicornous uterus (absence of one uterine horn); septate uteri (persistence of a septum or projecting wall between the two horns); and bicornuate uterus (presence of two separate uterine cavities leading to the same cervix, or complete duplication with two uteri each having its own cervix). These may or may not lead to infertility or repetitive spontaneous abortions, depending upon the extent of the problem and the ability of the uterus to enlarge sufficiently to accommodate the growing fetus. If a woman has experienced repeated second-trimester abortions and is diagnosed as having a Müllerian anomaly, reconstructive surgery may be attempted.

Uterine Tumors. The most common benign tumors of the uterus are leiomyomas, often called fibroids. These are thought to occur in 4 to 11 percent of women and be inconsequential in most. Where a causative relationship with reproductive casualty does exist, it is believed to be more a function of tumor location than of size. Masses which are in a position to seriously hamper fetal growth—by distorting the surface of the uterine wall or blocking the fallopian tubes and compromising the baby's blood supply—can in most cases be surgically removed. Despite the fact that they tend to enlarge rapidly under the influence of the hormones produced by the placenta, however, fibroids rarely cause significant problems in pregnancy.

Perinatal Death

The most widely recognized risk factor during late pregnancy is the presence of maternal disease. Diabetes mellitus, kidney disease, hypertension, heart disease, and lupus erythematosus are among the many conditions which may interfere with fetal growth and normal placental function. Because the compromising effects of poor maternal health on fetal status have been appreciated for so long, however, this has also been an area of great technological advancement. Says

Sheila Garvey, R.N., diabetic educator and author, with Donald R. Coustan, M.D., of the book, *The Baby Team:* "I warn the women I counsel not to be discouraged by old wives' tales. You can afford to be a 'tough-minded optimist.' Today, with realistic awareness of the dangers and a planned, carefully supervised pregnancy, the high-risk mother's chances of success are really excellent."

For example, administration of a drug called RhoGAM (Anti-RhO (D) immune globulin) within seventy-two hours of childbirth or an early termination of pregnancy can prevent development of Rh sensitization in nearly 100 percent of new mothers at risk, and greatly reduce the likelihood of intrauterine anemia and newborn jaundice in subsequent pregnancies. It is expected that Rh hemolytic disease, up to now a formidable threat to fetal/newborn life and health, may be almost totally eliminated by new methods of using such agents.

Among other specifically obstetrical complications, pregnancy-induced hypertension (toxemia) and abruption (premature detachment) of the placenta deserve special mention. Both strike hardest at the high-risk population and seem to recur in subsequent pregnancies. And then there is the vast gray area of fetal complication known as uteroplacental insufficiency, UPI, or placental dysfunction. Briefly summarized, UPI involves the inability of a prematurely aging placenta to supply the developing fetus with oxygen and nutrients. The baby's growth slows, sometimes with little or no warning. This may be followed by fetal distress and the death *in utero* of a small-for-gestational-age (SGA) infant.

If a baby's growth appears to be tapering off during the course of pregnancy, a variety of diagnostic procedures may be used to determine whether more aggressive treatment is required. These include: the oxytocin challenge test (OCT), which assesses the response of the fetal heart to the stress of uterine contractions; the nonstress test (NST), which evaluates heart-rate response to spontaneous fetal movement; ultrasound, to determine size and the relationship of head growth to body growth; and chemical evaluations of estriol excretion in maternal serum and/or urine.

Perinatal risk increases in relation to both maternal age and parity (number of surviving offspring), although as far as the latter is concerned the influence of societal factors (poverty, poor general health) is probably at least as significant as the number of pregnancies *per se.* Women who have experienced five or more pregnancies ("grand multipara" is the technical term) do tend to give birth precipitously, with increased complications of postpartum tissue damage and hemorrhage. Older women are also more vulnerable to complicating chronic disorders, such as diabetes and hypertension. As suggested earlier, women who experience conception difficulties and recurrent spontaneous abortions in their early to mid-twenties (the "ideal" reproductive age from a biological standpoint), and then succeed in carrying a pregnancy to viability in their late thirties or forties, are at some added risk of producing a low-birthweight infant.

Deaths occurring in the course of labor and delivery most often involve lack of oxygen due to cord compression, placental complications, birth injuries or "trauma," intrauterine infection, or the inability of a weakened infant to withstand the stress of labor as a result of gross congenital malformations.

Often multiple, overlapping factors are involved: for example, respiratory failure due to congenital heart disease in the immature infant of a diabetic mother. If the precise cause of death is unclear, "perinatal asphyxia" or "hypoxia" may be listed on the stillbirth certificate—a confusing practice which lumps conditions such as cord strangulation together with the multiple abnormalities that may eventually lead to fetal hypoxia.

Why Genetic Testing?

To reveal the presence of a suspected genetic abnormality in the fetus or heritable condition which could influence the outcome of future pregnancies . . . to recommend specific diagnostic and/or therapeutic measures in the event such an abnormality or condition exists, and provide reassurance, where it does not . . . and to help couples make informed choices about their reproductive options and acquaint them with the national, statewide, and community resources at their disposal, the March of Dimes Birth Defects Foundation began, in 1970, to support development of a network of genetic screening programs at medical centers throughout the country. At the present time, there are over a hundred full-service genetic testing and consultation centers in the United States, capable of providing help for thousands of couples annually.

Among the indications for referral to a medical genetics unit are:

- Family history of an inherited disorder
- Mental retardation or genetic anomaly in a surviving child or other family member

- History of repeated fetal losses and/or newborn deaths
- History of infertility
- Maternal age above thirty-five years
- Drug use or chronic exposure to toxic chemicals

Death of a Newborn

The same factors that contribute to fetal loss in the course of pregnancy and birth may also result in the death of a liveborn infant. Since 1915, the relative contribution of congenital malformations to infant mortality has risen dramatically (see table below), as other causes of death have declined in response to improved obstetrical care. Significantly, a high percentage of infants with congenital anomalies are also small for their gestational ages at birth.

Contribution of Congenital Malformations to Infant Deaths, U.S.A., 1915 to 1976 *

	1915	1976
Overall infant mortality rate (100,000 live births)	10,000	1,500
Infant deaths due to congenital malformations	640	260
Contribution of congenital malformations to death rate	6.4%	17.3%

* From *Antenatal Diagnosis*, NIH publication No. 79-1973, April 1979, p. I-27.

Immaturity, as judged by gestational age (under thirty-seven weeks) but even more accurately by birthweight, remains the single greatest cause of neonatal death, accounting for approximately 75 to 80 percent of all losses in the first month of life—this despite the fact that only 8 percent or so of newborns in the United States are classified as low-birthweight by the present criterion of weight equaling 2500 grams (5.5 pounds) or under. A disproportionately high number of immature births are the result of twin or other multiple pregnancies; only about 1 percent of pregnancies in the U.S. are twin pregnancies, yet these account for approximately 10 percent of all perinatal losses.

Other factors which may precipitate spontaneous preterm labor or delivery of a low-birthweight infant include: maternal systemic diseases such as diabetes, renal disease, heart disease, and hypertension; Rh sensitization; cervical incompetence or other uterine abnormality; infections of the urinary tract; other maternal infections, such as pneumonia; abruption of the placenta; placenta previa (abnormally low implantation of the placenta); and cigarette smoking.

Because of the clear association of gestational age with newborn survival and the large representation of low- and especially very low-birthweight infants (those weighing under 1,500 grams) among the early casualties, prevention of preterm labor and refinement of techniques of fetal surveillance and life support have been major goals of modern perinatal care. Currently, a group of muscle relaxants known as tocolytic agents are showing great promise for their capacity to arrest premature labor by inhibiting uterine muscle contractility. And once outside the uterus, smaller and smaller newborns—some weighing as little as one pound—are being successfully rescued from malnutrition, hypo- and hyperthermia, infection, and other perils.

A very dramatic milestone was the development, some years back, of a method of assessing fetal lung maturity by measuring the ratio of two chemicals of the phospholipid group, lecithin and sphingomyelin, in amniotic fluid. This procedure, first described by pediatrician Louis Gluck and his associates, allows the clinician to determine whether a threatened pregnancy can be safely interrupted (by induced labor or cesarean section), or whether doing so would only impose an additional risk of respiratory distress syndrome (RDS) on the already compromised fetus.

RDS, formerly known as hyaline membrane disease, is the leading killer of immature infants, whose respiratory passages tend to become clogged due to deficiency of a detergent-like material known as pulmonary surfactant. In some instances, administration of corticosteroid drugs can promote lung maturation in a preterm infant. Research is also underway to perfect a synthetic analogue of human pulmonary surfactant, manufactured from beef lung, which can be administered by tube to infants incapable of making their own.

Risks associated with postmaturity, or prolonged gestation beyond the expected forty-two-week interval, are also better understood, with the result that obstetricians are now paying greater attention to accurate pregnancy dating and identification of the approximately 30 percent of overdue pregnancies in which fetal post-

Guide to Major Perinatal Infections *

Infection in the mother	Mode of transmission	Hazards in the first trimester	Hazards in the second trimester
VIRAL			
Rubella	Transplacental. Causes congenital rubella; postnatal infection may cause rubella in newborn.	Greatest danger. Fetus may develop gross anomalies and developmental defects. Intervention: Therapeutic abortion.	Probably none, but hearing loss possible.
Cytomegalovirus (CMV)	Transplacental. May cause congenital infection. Local lesions in birth canal may cause infection in newborn.	Unknown. Some evidence suggests may be serious.	May be serious, resulting in multiple defects and developmental abnormalities.
Varicella (chickenpox)	Transplacental. May cause congenital lesions in birth canal, or nose/mouth, or contact may cause varicella in newborn.	Rare, but some cases seen with special syndrome involving scarring of the skin, damage of the brain and eyes.	Not usually serious. But fetus may have varicella in utero and develop herpes zoster at an early age.
Herpes simplex (HSV)	Transplacental. May cause congenital infection; lesions in birth canal may cause infection to newborn.	Infection rare. If it occurs, eye and central nervous system (CNS) damage may result.	Maternal viremia may lead to severe defects in fetus.
Hepatitis B	Transplacental. May cause congenital hepatitis B.; postnatal infection may cause hepatitis in newborn.	Not a hazard	Fetus may be at some risk
PROTOZOAL			
Toxoplasmosis	Transplacental. May cause congenital toxoplasmosis.	Probably no hazard	May acquire infection
BACTERIAL			
Group B streptococcal infections	No transmission until after membranes are ruptured or after delivery.	No hazard	No hazard
Gram-negative bacterial infections	No transmission until after membranes are ruptured or after delivery.	No hazard	No hazard
Congenital syphilis	Transplacental. May cause congenital syphilis; lesions in birth canal may cause syphilis in newborn.	Mother may deliver a stillborn infant.	Infection with congenital syphilis may occur.

* From Charlotte Isler, "Infection: Constant Threat to Perinatal Life," *RN* 38:8 (August 1975), pp. 26-27.

Hazards in the third trimester	Delivery and immediate neonatal period	Followup period and childhood	Prevention or treatment for mother, neonate, child.
Probably none	If infected during the first trimester, severe anomalies result: cardiac defects, deafness, meningoencephalitis, eye defects, immunoglobulin deficiency, low birthweight, stillbirth.	Infant may shed virus up until one year of age. Mental retardation may not be a static process. Apparent mental retardation at age four may diminish or disappear by age nine and up. Diabetes, hyperthyroidism, or precocious puberty may show in later childhood.	Prevention: Immunization of mother more than three months before start of pregnancy. Massive immunization of children.
May contract infection, remain asymptomatic.	May be asymptomatic or uninfected until passing through birth canal. If infected during second trimester, may have brain damage, retardation, liver disease, cerebral palsy, cardiac, eye, ear, and other defects.	If CMV is contracted during the third trimester, hearing impairment, diminished intelligence, immune system deficiency, behavioral disturbances, or learning disabilities may result.	Various antiviral agents now under study, none highly successful to date. Are very toxic. Include cytosine arabinoside (ARA-C), adenine arabinoside (ARA-A), and iododioxiuridine (IDUR).
Serious hazard if mother develops varicella four days or less prior to delivery. Infant may develop severe or fatal varicella unless given zoster immune globulin immediately after birth.	In congenital varicella, infant may have skin, brain, and eye damage.	If infection is mild or modified, no sequelae may persist. If infected in utero, infant may develop herpes zoster at an early age.	Modification: If mother contracts infection four days or less prior to delivery, zoster immune globulin is given to the infant immediately after delivery.
Infection may occur through contact with contaminated internal fetal monitor. Cesarean section may be done prior to the rupture of membranes to prevent infection.	Infection may occur in birth canal. Central nervous system defects may result. Severe infection may kill the infant.	Chorioretinitis may develop. CNS defects persist if present at birth. Local herpes lesions may develop.	Same as for CMV
Fetus is at greatest risk if infected at this time.	Infant may be asymptomatic, but act as a carrier. Jaundice and hepatosplenomegaly may develop.	Jaundice and hepatosplenomegaly may develop. Infant may die of serious infection. Liver damage or portal fibrosis may develop. Infant may become a long-term carrier.	Experimental vaccine has been developed, but is not yet available.
May acquire infection. Premature labor, intrauterine growth retardation.	May be subclinical or asymptomatic, but may show a positive lab finding. May be born with congenital toxoplasmosis, have only mild disease, or show symptoms such as growth retardation.	In severe sequelae, may develop cerebrospinal fluid abnormalities, immune deficiencies, hearing and eye defects, intracranial calcification, or hepatosplenomegaly. Intelligence may be lowered in later childhood.	Pyrimethamine (an antiprotozoal agent)
No hazard until after membranes rupture.	May develop serious, often fatal early-onset disease within one week of birth. Infection may show up as septicemia, pneumonia, meningitis, empyema. Usually due to Group B strep. serotypes la, lb, lc and ll. Early-onset disease is usually transmitted from mother to newborn; late-onset disease by hospital personnel.	May develop late-onset disease. Milder than early-onset disease, and mortality rate is lower. Caused usually by Group B strep serotype lll.	Penicillin
No hazard until after membranes rupture.	Infection may be acquired within 48 hours after birth. Anaerobic organisms may be acquired at same time. Results in neonatal sepsis or sepsis with complications, such as meningitis.	Diagnosis generally certain by age of 2 weeks.	Ampicillin and gentamicin parenterally and intrathecally.
Infection may occur. Congenital syphilis will result.	May be infected during delivery from lesions in birth canal of untreated infected mother, or may show symptoms of congenital syphilis	If congenital syphilis is present, infant has lesions of long bones, eats poorly, may have jaundice, elevated temperature, nasal discharge (snuffles) and peeling rash.	Prevention: treating mother prior to or during pregnancy with penicillin. Congenital syphilis or acute syphilitic lesions treated with penicillin can eradicate disease in infant if treatment started early.

maturity syndrome associated with placental aging is likely to develop.

Occasionally, an underlying congenital anomaly such as anencephaly will result in a post-dates pregnancy. More often, the baby is totally normal in appearance, although relatively thin and covered with dry, peeling skin due to the absence of lubricating vernix. As the placenta ages, there is marked impairment of blood supply to the fetus and a resultant reduction in the transfer of oxygen and nutrients. Because the weakened baby has difficulty meeting the demands of labor and delivery, perinatal mortality associated with postmaturity syndrome is between two and three times that of term labor. In addition, there is an increased (perhaps by as much as 50 percent) tendency for future pregnancies to be similarly prolonged. Despite these handicaps, with availability of modern tools for maternal-fetal assessment, the option of cesarean section when the baby is already compromised and the cervix is unripe, and access to newborn intensive-care services, the outlook for postmature infants has begun to improve.

Prompt referral of pre- and postterm, low-birthweight, and critically ill newborns to regional perinatal centers for intensive care is generally credited with the recent, rapid decline in neonatal mortality—from 20 per 1000 live births in 1950 to 8.5 per 1000 live births in 1980. Although three-quarters of this decline occurred in the ten-year period following institution of vigilant perinatal care, there is some disagreement over the role played by refined technology in altering pregnancy outcome. It is pointed out that casualty rates have also dropped at those institutions where elaborate diagnostic equipment is generally unavailable, a trend which suggests that improved economic conditions and changes in the childbearing population may be the hidden variables. The latter include increased availability of family planning services, safe abortion, and the resulting tendency of couples to limit family size and space pregnancies farther apart, which in turn lowers the incidence of multiple births and low-birthweight infants.

VICTIMS OF ECONOMIC BLIGHT

Despite recent medical breakthroughs and improvements in the organization and availability of health services, however, the United

States continues to lag behind a dozen or so other nations in its ability to safeguard perinatal life and health. Even more disheartening is the gap in obstetrical outcomes which still exists between rich and poor, black and white in the U.S. In a study conducted jointly by the University of California School of Public Health and the Information Sciences Research Institute in Washington, D.C., mortality rates for other-than-white infants, although declining proportionately faster, exceeded white rates by over 60 percent, and rates in rural areas were consistently higher than those in urban areas. Other studies have shown that the incidence of low-birthweight babies has actually *increased* among nonwhite mothers during the past ten years, at a time when neonatal mortality was declining for all racial groups. According to the National Center for Health Statistics, black infants are more than twice as likely as white infants to be born prematurely.

Both poverty and race have also been shown to correlate with placental dysfunction and prenatal infection. An analysis by pathologists Richard L. Naeye and William A. Blanc of 1,044 consecutive autopsies of stillborn and newborn infants at Babies Hospital in New York indicated that, of the 27 percent who demonstrated congenital pneumonia or sepsis,* infants from poor families had about twice the rate of infection of infants from more prosperous families and black infants about double the rate of whites and Puerto Ricans. While other reports have suggested differing standards of institutional prenatal care as being primarily responsible for the higher mortality rates of infants from poor families, Naeye and Blanc point out that in their study, factors outside the hospital environment appeared to be implicated: "Different economic and racial groups receiving care in the same prenatal clinic had quite different rates of antenatal infection. Such differences were also found in newborn infants whose mothers had received prenatal care at a wide variety of medical institutions and clinics throughout the New York City area." [2]

Genetic influences, possibly related to poor maternal nutrition over many generations, and young maternal age are likely culprits. These are often connected: There is a tendency for pregnant teenagers—especially those under fifteen years of age—to be both inadequately nourished and reluctant to take advantage of available prenatal services, including dietary counseling. Very young pregnant patients are also at higher risk for development of pregnancy-induced

---

* Primarily related to the aspiration of infected amniotic fluid.

hypertension and labor difficulties, and more likely to give birth to premature and/or low-birthweight infants. Despite these problems, a 1978 report showed that *nearly 20 percent of expectant mothers under fifteen years of age received little or no prenatal care at all.*

"There is considerable evidence that the social influences affecting low birthweight and other causes of perinatal mortality have their greatest impact during the mother's own developmental years," sums up Jan Schneider, M.D., chairman of the department of obstetrics and gynecology at The Medical College of Pennsylvania, in Philadelphia. "Although childhood patterns of deprivation are often difficult to isolate from similar processes later on," says Dr. Schneider, "early poverty and malnutrition probably have a lifelong influence upon reproductive potential. It is significant that the same list of factors associated with increased newborn mortality tend also to be associated with higher fetal death rates."

THE GOVERNMENT STEPS IN

To improve delivery of perinatal-care services to those high-risk mothers most in need of them, the following federal government programs have been put into effect:

In 1963, Maternal and Child Health and Mental Retardation amendments to title V of the Social Security Act authorized the setting up of Maternity and Infant Care (MIC) projects in areas with the highest maternal and infant mortality rates. Ultimately, MIC projects were established at fifty-six sites, in thirty-four states, the District of Columbia, and Puerto Rico.

The aim of the projects was to provide broad-based care by an interdisciplinary health team for women during pregnancy, labor, delivery, and the postpartum period, and infant care during the first year of life. Included were such areas as nutritional counseling, family planning, nursing services, and transportation, as well as basic medical and dental care. Despite this impressive-sounding list, a 1974* article in *Public Health Reports* commented: "It is evident that the MIC Projects are reaching only a small percentage of high-risk maternity patients—the 117,314 patients who received care [in fiscal year 1974] represent only about 15 percent of an estimated 750,000 high-risk patients delivered each year." [3]

* The year in which administration of the projects was turned over to the individual states.

In 1977, additional federal funds were authorized, again under title V of the Social Security Act, to aid thirteen high-priority states (most in the southern United States) in establishing regional perinatal services. Currently, the Improve Pregnancy Outcome program, as it is called, has been expanded to cover twenty-three states in all. Funds are used to provide both regional and local maternity care, including identification of high-risk pregnancies and high-risk infants and outreach programs aimed at pregnant teenagers.

More recently, concern that the nationwide programs emphasizing regionalization have begun to encourage costly overlapping of intensive-care services has prompted a third variety of government legislation—this time, directly involving the consumers of health care. In 1978, implementation of an older law, the 1974 Health Planning Resources Development Act, made it mandatory for concerned citizens to have an opportunity to participate with health professionals in the planning of strategies to meet local community health needs. How this will affect the changing picture of reproductive casualty in the United States has yet to be determined, but it is hoped that at least part of the consumer effort will be aimed at channeling government spending away from costly, last-ditch interventions and toward more basic preventive health care for all expectant mothers.

"The heightened interest in preventive medicine stems from our progressive disillusionment with the curative approach," says Dr. Calvin J. Hobel of Los Angeles County Harbor-UCLA Medical Center.[4] Writing in The Lancet, Hobel proposes that future perinatal research focus on three major preventive areas: (1) identification of the characteristics of pregnancies at risk for preterm labor; (2) early management of intrauterine fetal growth retardation; and (3) further investigation of the genetic causes of fetal and infant loss.

The fact is that we already have the technical capacity to make substantial inroads in all three areas—as well as to take public and private action against the environmental contaminants which pose an increasing threat to fetal outcome. But prevention is only as effective as the programs used to implement it. And to be really effective, it should be thought about not when the expectant mother is already twenty or thirty years old, but when she is a child herself. "The need for instruction about health, conception, pregnancy, and child spacing ideally should start early in the preschool years and continue throughout life," observes perinatologist Jan Schneider. "All individuals should learn of the value of postponement of the first pregnancy until conditions of health and socioeconomic status are favorable, of the importance of child spacing and of the need for regular health care. Such teaching must be supported and backed by the availability of good health care including family planning services, prenatal care and interconceptional care." [5]

Poverty, malnutrition, and inadequate prenatal care are factors which predispose even young and otherwise healthy women to pregnancy loss. Until families of all economic strata gain access to genetic testing and modern perinatal health services, any talk of reducing reproductive casualties to a minimum will remain merely talk.

Afterword

"LOSING THE BABY made me reassess everything: my religious beliefs, my values, my marriage, my friendships. Everything got turned upside down, and some things fell back into place while others didn't. . . ." "Within a year after my miscarriage, I had gotten divorced, moved out of my apartment, and begun a long, involved affair with somebody else. When I try to imagine what my life would have been like if the baby had lived—I can't. I'm a different person now. . . ." "You learn to weigh things differently. Today, a walk with my little girl is more important than whether or not the dishes get done."

Psychosocial crises are times when we reassess our relationship with the world and emerge with what Colin Murray Parkes calls "major changes in the heartland of self." After a loss in pregnancy there is pain and confusion, and the death not only of the wished-for child, but of the parents' dreams and hopes for it and for themselves, as well. And there is an unexpected loss of illusion: about one's self, one's partner, one's friends. Things will never be the same. There is no going back. But there can be growth and a new compassion. One woman recalled going out into the garden a few weeks after her baby's death, and wondering how it could be that I had ever worried about the weeds, when there were children dying of malnutrition all over the world.

"Just as broken bones may end up stronger than unbroken ones," says Parkes, "so the experience of grieving can strengthen and bring maturity to those who have previously been protected from misfortune. The pain of grief is just as much a part of life as the joy of love; it is, perhaps, the price we pay for love, the cost of commitment." [1]

Whether it results in a live birth or not, each new pregnancy is such a commitment.

Appendix: Parent Support Groups

THIS LISTING, ADAPTED from the brochure of P.E.P.D. (Parents Experiencing Perinatal Death), provides examples of the specific services a parent support group can perform in the community. Following it are the names and addresses of some of the more established organizations. Several have branches elsewhere. Check your local hospital, health department, or mental health center to see whether such a group may be forming in your area.

SERVICES OF A SUPPORT GROUP

- Suggesting ways to help other children and family members cope with the loss.
- Preparing parents for receiving autopsy results and death certificate by mail, as well as baby products from advertisers, etc.
- Outlining health department procedures for moving the baby to the county cemetery.
- Providing home or hospital visitation on request.
- Having mothers and fathers who have experienced perinatal death available by telephone twenty-four hours a day, to listen and reassure parents of the normalcy of grief reactions.
- Training "Listening Parents" to perform this service.
- Helping parents consider alternatives concerning future children; preparing them for possible anxieties during future pregnancies.
- Holding informal neighborhood meetings.
- Fulfilling speaking requests from hospitals, churches, and public

151

agencies, and holding city-wide meetings on such topics as symptoms and stages of grief, burial problems, and genetic testing and counseling.

• Educating mental health centers, family counseling agencies, and crisis centers concerning the particular needs of parents experiencing perinatal death.

ORGANIZATIONS

THE SOCIETY OF
COMPASSIONATE FRIENDS
International Headquarters:
109 Lillington Road
Leamington Spa,
Warwickshire, England CV32 6LJ
(over 270 branches throughout the U.S.)

U.S. Headquarters
P. O. Box 1347
Oak Brook, IL 60521

In California:

S.A.N.D.
c/o Janet Kirksey
Alta Bates Hospital
Berkeley, CA 94705

A.M.E.N.D.
4032 Towhee Drive
Calabassas, CA 91302

R.E.S.P.O.N.D.
c/o Kathy Sorrels

10 Forest Creek Circle
Chico, CA 95926

S.H.A.R.E.
c/o Diana Brenseth
5854 East Lansing
Fresno, CA 93727

H.A.N.D.
c/o Ginger Valen
19 West Gate Way
San Anselmo, CA 94960

In Colorado:

BOULDER COUNTY STILLBORN/
NEWBORN LOSS SUPPORT GROUP
Boulder County Hospice
Boulder, CO 80302

ROSE MEDICAL CENTER
Attn: Mary Krugman, Coordinator
Parent Education Program
4567 East Ninth Avenue
Denver. CO 80220

In Connecticut:

BEREAVED PARENTS
c/o Nancy Baranowski

28 Wesley Drive
Huntington, CT 06484

In Florida:

H.O.P.E.S.
c/o Sandi Poston
P.O. Box 1143
Lutz, FL 33549

A.M.E.N.D.
c/o Dottie Cannon
5104 127th Avenue
Tampa, FL 33617

In Illinois:

A.M.E.N.D.
c/o Jane Borman
2209 Gillis
Alton, IL 62002

S.H.A.R.E.
St. Elizabeth's Hospital
Pastoral Care Department
211 South 3rd Street
Belleville, IL 62221

S.H.A.R.E.
Memorial Hospital of Carbondale
404 West Main Street
Carbondale, IL 62901

S.H.A.R.E.
St. Anthony Hospital
503 Maple Street
Effingham, IL 62401

S.H.A.R.E.
Passavant Area Hospital
1600 West Walnut Street
Jacksonville, IL 62650

S.H.A.R.E.
St. Francis Hospital
1215 East Union
Litchfield, IL 62056

S.H.A.R.E.
Gregory and Joanne Matzke
10301 Medill
Melrose Park, IL 60164
  (Chicago area)

P.A.C.E.S.
Bereaved Parents
c/o Cathy McMeilly
619 South Humphrey
Oak Park, IL 60304

S.H.A.R.E.
St. Francis Hospital Medical Center
530 N.E. Glen Oak
Peoria, IL 61637

S.H.A.R.E.
Blessing Hospital
1005 Broadway
Quincy, IL 62301
  or
St. Mary's Hospital
1415 Vermont
Quincy, IL 62301

S.H.A.R.E.
Rockford Memorial Hospital
2400 North Rockton
Rockford, IL 61103

S.H.A.R.E.
c/o Sister Jane Marie Lamb
St. John's Hospital
800 East Carpenter
Springfield, IL 62702

S.H.A.R.E.
c/o Sandra D. Dunn
Mercy Hospital
1400 West Park
Urbana, IL 61801

In Indiana:

BEREAVED PARENTS GROUP
Parents and Friends of Children
c/o Linda Runden
622 North Capitol Avenue
Corydon, IN 47112

PROJECT COMFORT
c/o Gerald C. Machgan, Chaplain

Parkview Hospital
2200 Randalia Drive
Fort Wayne, IN 46805

NEO FIGHT
c/o Pam Dickerson
4815 North Kenyon Drive
Indianapolis, IN 46226

In Iowa:

EMPTY ARMS
c/o Dr. Russell Striffler
St. Luke's Methodist Hospital

1026 A. Avenue, N.E.
Cedar Rapids, IA 52402

In Kansas:

BEREAVED PARENTS OF
PITTSBURG
c/o Mrs. Howard Thompson

Quincy & Bypass
Pittsburg, KS 66762

In Kentucky:

NORTON-CHILDREN'S HOSPITAL
c/o Chaplain Wayne Willis

P.O. Box 35070
Louisville, KY 40232

In Massachusetts:

BOSTON HOSPITAL FOR WOMEN
Attn: Anne Groves, Director
Social Services
221 Longwood Avenue
Boston, MA 02115

C.O.P.E.
37 Clarendon Street
Boston, MA 02116

HOPE
c/o Susan Harrington
South Shore Hospital
55 Fogg Road
South Weymouth, MA 02190

BOSTON STILLBIRTH
STUDY GROUP
c/o Ann Ross, Jean Stringham, and
Judith Riley
53 Country Corners Road
Wayland, MA 01778

GRIEF SUPPORT GROUP
Childbirth Education Association of
Central Massachusetts
c/o Linda Brink and Merilyn Bambauer
P.O. Box 193, West Side Station
Worcester, MA 01602

In Michigan:

P.E.N.D.
c/o Neonatal I.C.U. Marcia Eager
Butterworth Hospital
Grand Rapids, MI 49503

SURVIVORS-UP FROM GRIEF
17125 Fordline
Riverview, MI 48192

BEREAVED PARENTS GROUP
c/o Betty Rabaut
St. Bede's Church
18290 W. Twelve Mile Road
Southfield, MI 48076

In Minnesota:

PARENTS' GRIEF SUPPORT GROUP
c/o Judy Zehren
Route 1 Box 2006
Britt, MN 55710

PARENTS' GRIEF SUPPORT GROUP
c/o Kathy Peterson
St. Mary's Hospital
Duluth, MN 55805

In Missouri:

PARENTS IN CRISIS
c/o Sue Hiesten
303 Brewer
Columbia, MO 65201

MOTHERS-IN-CRISIS
c/o Terry Weston
Social Services Department
Freeman Hospital
Joplin, MO 64801

A.M.E.N.D.
c/o Maureen Connelly

4324 Berrywick
St. Louis, MO 63128

In New Jersey:

HELP
c/o Eileen Thompson
Ventnor, NJ 08406

In New York:

BEREAVEMENT CLINIC
c/o Joanne Middleton
Downstate Medical Center
450 Clarkson Avenue
Brooklyn, NY 11203

S.H.A.R.E.
c/o Lois Sugarman

6726 Gleason Place
Fayetteville, NY 13066

MISCARRIAGE AND STILLBIRTH
SUPPORT GROUP
c/o Dorothy Hai
209 York Street
Olean, NY 14760

In North Carolina:

PARENT CARE, INC.
c/o Lil Galphin
Box 125
Cary, NC 27511

KINDER-MOURN, INC
605 East Boulevard
Charlotte, NC 28203

In Ohio:

BEREAVED PARENTS GROUP
3136 Ellet Avenue
Akron, OH 44312

P.E.N.D.
Rainbow Babies and Children's Hospital
2101 Adelbert Road
Cleveland, OH 44106

S.H.A.R.E.
Marilyn Miller Graef
1272 Indian Hill Drive
Bolivar, OH 44612

PARENT SUPPORT GROUP
Childbirth Education Association of Akron
c/o Linda Baily
2183 Larchdale
Guy Falls, OH 44221

In Oklahoma:

A.M.E.N.D.
1344 East 26th Place
Tulsa, OK 74100

In Pennsylvania:

S.H.A.R.E.
P.O. Box 961
Lancaster, PA 17604

BOOTH MATERNITY HOSPITAL
GRIEF PROCESS GROUP
c/o Dr. Nancy Johns and Laurie Rendall

In Pennsylvania:

6051 Overbrook Avenue
Philadelphia, PA 19131

GRIEVING CLINIC
c/o Dr. Susan Jasin
Temple University Health Sciences Center

3401 North Broad Street
Philadelphia, PA 19140

U.N.I.T.E.
7600 Central Avenue
Philadelphia, PA 19111

In Tennessee:

P.E.P.D.
P.O. Box 38445
Germantown, TN 38138

In Texas:

H.O.P.E.
c/o Karen Riley
14207 Locke Lane
Houston, TX 77077

S.H.A.R.E. OF SAN ANTONIO
The Harbor
3534 Avenue B
San Antonio, TX 78209

In Utah:

SHARING HEART
c/o Thomas D. Coleman
University of Utah Medical Center

Department of Pediatrics, Room 2B425
50 North Medical Drive
Salt Lake City, UT 84132

In Washington:

PARENTS OF STILLBORNS
Group Health Cooperative-East Side
Redmond, WA 98052

PARENTS OF STILLBORNS
c/o Bill and Doreen Dolleman
6210 South 120th Street
Seattle, WA 98178

In Wisconsin:

S.H.A.R.E.
St. Vincent Hospital
P.O. Box 1220
Green Bay, WI 54305

S.H.A.R.E.
St. Francis Medical Center
700 West Avenue South
LaCrosse, WI 54601
          or
Lutheran Hospital
1910 South Avenue
LaCrosse, WI 54601

BEREAVED PARENTS
SUPPORT GROUP
c/o Carol Fowler

1016 Van Buren Street
Madison, WI 53711

AIID
Childbirth Education Association
5636 West Burleigh
Milwaukee, WI 53210

S.H.A.R.E.
St. Nicholas Hospital
2419 Saemann Avenue
Sheboygan, WI 53081

PARENTS SUPPORTING PARENTS
c/o Rice Clinic
Mary Berg, R.N.
2501 Main Street
Stevens Point, WI 54481

For couples facing additional infertility problems:

RESOLVE, INC.
P.O. Box 474
Belmont, MA 02178

Notes

1. THE COUPLE'S RESPONSE

1. Gerald Caplan, "The Mental Hygiene Role of the Nurse in Maternal and Child Care," *Nursing Outlook*, 1954, p. 14, quoted in: Judith E. Buxton and A. Courtney McKay, "The Effects of a Woman's Unsuccessful Reproductive History on Emotional Stress in a Subsequent Pregnancy" (Boston University School of Nursing, Aug. 1968), p. 2.
2. D. Gary Benfield, Susan A. Leib, and John H. Vollman, "Grief Response of Parents to Neonatal Death and Parent Participation in Deciding Care," *Pediatrics* 62:2 (August 1978), p. 171.
3. J. Cullberg, "Mental Reactions of Women to Perinatal Death," *Psychosomatic Medicine in Obstetrics and Gynaecology*, 3rd International Congress, London 1971 (Basel, Switz.: Karger, 1972), p. 326.
4. Ibid.
5. Colin Murray Parkes, *Bereavement: Studies of Grief in Adult Life* (New York: International Universities Press, Inc., 1972), p. 121.
6. Andrew D. Elia, "The Management of Grief Situations in Obstetrics," *The Boston Medical Quarterly* 10:1 (March 1959).
7. Emanuel Lewis, "The Management of Stillbirth: Coping With an Unreality," *The Lancet*, September 18, 1976, p. 620.
8. Ann S. Kliman, *Crisis: Psychological First Aid for Recovery and Growth* (New York: Holt, Rinehart and Winston, 1978), p. 5.
9. Robert Frost, *The Poetry of Robert Frost*, ed. Edward Connery Lathem (New York: Holt, Rinehart and Winston, 1969), pp. 51-55.
10. Marshall H. Klaus and John H. Kennell, *Maternal-Infant Bonding: The Impact of Early Separation or Loss on Family Development* (St. Louis: The C.V. Mosby Company, 1976), p. 225.
11. Harriet Sarnoff Schiff, *The Bereaved Parent* (Harmondsworth, Middlesex, Engl.: Penguin Books, 1977), p. 58.

157

2. THE COMMUNITY'S RESPONSE

1. Louise J. Kaplan, *Oneness and Separateness: From Infant to Individual* (New York: Simon and Schuster, 1978), p. 45.
2. Robert Fulton, "On the Dying of Death," in Earl A. Grollman, ed., *Explaining Death to Children* (Boston: Beacon Press, 1967), p. 45.
3. Ibid., p. 46.
4. Elisabeth Kübler-Ross, *On Death and Dying* (New York: Macmillan Publishing Co., Inc., 1969), p. 15.
5. Geoffrey Gorer, *Death, Grief, and Mourning* (Garden City, N.Y.: Doubleday and Company, Inc., 1965), p. 128.
6. Ernest Becker, *The Denial of Death* (New York: The Free Press, 1973), ix.
7. Emanuel Lewis, "The Management of Stillbirth: Coping with an Unreality," p. 619.
8. William Kotzwinkle, *Swimmer in the Secret Sea* (New York: Avon Books, 1975), p. 42.
9. Sherron Hughes-Tremper and Barbara Nelson, "On the Death of an Infant," information booklet, Lutheran General Hospital, Park Ridge, Ill.
10. Colin Murray Parkes, *Bereavement: Studies of Grief in Adult Life*, p. 163.
11. Gorer, p. xxxiii.
12. Marion Cohen, "This Is What I Do With Kerin," *Mothering*, Fall 1980, p. 89.
13. Ibid.
14. Ibid.

3. MOTHERS' VOICES: THE WORK OF MOURNING

1. C. S. Lewis, *A Grief Observed* (New York: The Seabury Press, 1961), p. 47.
2. Erich Lindemann, "Symptomatology and Management of Acute Grief," *American Journal of Psychiatry* 101 (September 1944), p. 141.
3. Ibid., p. 145.
4. Ibid., p. 143.
5. Colin Murray Parkes, *Bereavement: Studies of Grief in Adult Life*, p. 39.
6. Ibid., p. 37.
7. Ibid., p. 85.
8. Lewis, pp. 24-26.
9. Marion Cohen, "This Is What I Do With Kerin," p. 89.
10. Harriet Sarnoff Schiff, *The Bereaved Parent*, p. 21.
11. Cohen, p. 89.
12. Steven Moss, "The Grief Work Cycle in Judaism," in Irwin Gerber *et al.*, eds., *Perspectives on Bereavement* (New York: Arno Press, 1979), p. 173.
13. Schiff, p. 127.
14. Ibid.
15. Earl A. Grollman, "The Ritualistic and Theological Approach of the Jew," in

Earl A. Grollman, ed., *Explaining Death to Children* (Boston: Beacon Press, 1967), p. 231.

4. THE CAREGIVER'S RESPONSE

1. Marshall H. Klaus and John H. Kennell, *Maternal-Infant Bonding*, p. 214.
2. Andrew D. Elia, "The Management Of Grief Situations in Obstetrics."
3. Ibid.
4. Ronald J. Knapp and Larry G. Peppers, "Doctor-Patient Relationships in Fetal/ Infant Death Encounters," *Journal of Medical Education* 54 (October 1979), p. 775.
5. Lewis Thomas, "Dying As Failure," *Annals of the American Academy of Political and Social Science* 447 (January 1980), p. 2.
6. Yasuo Ishida, "How to Deal with Grief in Childbirth," *The Female Patient* 5 (May 1980), p. 74.
7. Ronna Case, "When Birth Is Also a Funeral," *The Journal of Pastoral Care* 32:1 (March 1978), p. 16.
8. Pauline M. Seitz and Louise H. Warrick, "Perinatal Death: The Grieving Mother," *American Journal of Nursing* 74:11 (November 1974), p. 2029.
9. Ronald I. Clyman, Charlotte Green, Cynthia Mikkelsen, Jane Rowe, and Linda Ataide, "Do Parents Utilize Physician Follow-Up After the Death of Their Newborn?" *Pediatrics* 64:5 (November 1979), p. 665.
10. Ibid.
11. Anne Scupholme, "Who Helps? Coping with the Unexpected Outcomes of Pregnancy," *Journal of Obstetric, Gynecologic, and Neonatal Nursing*, July/ August 1978, p. 38.
12. Ibid.
13. Harriet Sarnoff Schiff, *The Bereaved Parent*, p. 14.

5. CHILDREN: THE FORGOTTEN MOURNERS

1. Robert Kastenbaum, "The Child's Understanding of Death: How Does It Develop?" in Earl A. Grollman, ed., *Explaining Death to Children* (Boston: Beacon Press, 1967), p. 99.
2. Ernest Becker, *The Denial of Death*, p. 18.
3. Gilbert W. Kliman and Albert Rosenfeld, *Responsible Parenthood: The Child's Psyche Through the Six-Year Pregnancy* (New York: Holt, Rinehart and Winston, 1980), p. 260.
4. Carol Hardgrove and Louise H. Warrick, "How Shall We Tell the Children?" *American Journal of Nursing* 74:3 (March 1974), p. 448.
5. Erna P. Furman, "The Death of a Newborn: Care of the Parents," *Birth and the Family Journal* 5:4 (Winter 1978), p. 214.
6. Marshall H. Klaus and John H. Kennell, *Maternal-Infant Bonding*, p. 220.
7. Edgar N. Jackson, "The Theological, Psychological, and Philosophical Dimen-

sions of Death in Protestantism," in Earl A. Grollman, ed., *Explaining Death to Children*, p. 180.

8. Elva Orlow Poznanski, "The 'Replacement Child': A Saga of Unresolved Parental Grief," *The Journal of Pediatrics* 81:6 (December 1972), p. 1192.

9. Colin Murray Parkes, *Bereavement: Studies of Grief in Adult Life*, p. 179.

6. LOOKING AHEAD

1. John R. Wolff, Paul E. Nielson, and Patricia Schiller, "The Emotional Reaction to a Stillbirth," *American Journal of Obstetrics and Gynecology* 108:1 (September 1, 1970), p. 73.

2. Ibid.

3. Jane Rowe, Ronald Clyman, Charlotte Green, Cynthia Mikkelsen, Jeanette Haight, and Linda Ataide, "Follow-Up of Families Who Experience Perinatal Death," *Pediatrics* 62:2 (August 1978), p. 166.

4. Ibid.

5. Pauline M. Seitz and Louise H. Warrick, "Perinatal Death: The Grieving Mother," p. 2033.

7. SEARCHING FOR ANSWERS

1. Silvio Aladjem, ed., *Risks in the Practice of Modern Obstetrics*, 2nd ed. (St. Louis: The C. V. Mosby Company, 1975), p. 27.

2. Richard L. Naeye and William A. Blanc, "Relation of Poverty and Race to Antenatal Infection," *New England Journal of Medicine* 283:11 (September 10, 1970), p. 559.

3. Helen M. Wallace, "Status of Infant and Perinatal Morbidity and Mortality: A Review of the Literature," *Public Health Reports* 93:4 (July–August 1978), p. 386.

4. Calvin J. Hobel, "Better Perinatal Health: U.S.A.," *The Lancet*, January 5, 1980, p. 33.

5. Jan Schneider, "Repeated Pregnancy Loss," *Clinical Obstetrics and Gynecology*, March 1973, p. 131.

AFTERWORD

1. Colin Murray Parkes, *Bereavement: Studies of Grief in Adult Life*, p. 5.

Bibliography

"A Matter of Birth and Death." *Emergency Medicine,* January 1978, pp. 37-39.

"The Abhorrence of Stillbirth." *The Lancet,* June 4, 1977, pp. 1188-90.

"Abnormal Infants of Diabetic Mothers." *The Lancet,* March 22, 1980, pp. 633-38.

Aladjem, Silvio, ed. *Risks in the Practice of Modern Obstetrics.* 2nd ed., St. Louis: The C.V. Mosby Company, 1975.

Alberman, Eva. "Prospects for Better Perinatal Health." *The Lancet,* January 26, 1980, pp. 189-92.

Alberman, Eva and Creasy, M.R. "Frequency of Chromosomal Abnormalities in Miscarriages and Perinatal Deaths." *The Journal of Medical Genetics* 14 (1977), pp. 313-15.

"Amniotic-Fluid Alpha-Fetoprotein Measurement in Antenatal Diagnosis of Anencephaly and Open Spina Bifida in Early Pregnancy," Second Report of the U. K. Collaborative Study on Alpha-Fetoprotein in Relation to Neural-Tube Defects. *The Lancet,* September 29, 1979, pp. 651-61.

Anderson, John Gordon, "Prayer—Upon the Death of an Infant." *The Journal of Pastoral Care* 32:1 (March 1978), p. 34.

Annis, Linda Ferrill. *The Child Before Birth.* Ithaca: Cornell University Press, 1978.

Antenatal Diagnosis: Report of a Consensus Development Conference Sponsored by the National Institute of Child Health and Human Development, Assisted by the Office for Medical Applications of Research and the Fogarty International Center, March 5-7, 1979. N.I.H., Bethesda, Md. N.I.H. Publication No. 79-1973 (April 1979).

Aubry, Richard H. and Pennington, John C. "Identification and Evaluation of High-Risk Pregnancy: The Perinatal Concept." *Clinical Obstetrics and Gynecology* 16:1 (March 1973).

"The Bad Egg." *The Lancet,* March 29, 1980, p. 690.

Banta, David and Thacker, Stephen. "Electronic Fetal Monitoring: Is It of Benefit?" *Birth and the Family Journal* 6:4 (Winter 1979), pp. 237-48.

Beard, R.W. and Rivers, R.P.A. "Fetal Asphyxia in Labour," *The Lancet*, November 24, 1979, pp. 1117-19.

Becker, Ernest. *The Denial of Death.* New York: The Free Press, 1973.

Benfield, D. Gary, Leib, Susan A., and Reuter, Jeanette. "Grief Response of Parents After Referral of the Critically Ill Newborn to a Regional Center." *The New England Journal of Medicine* 294:18 (April 29, 1976), pp. 975-78.

Benfield, D. Gary, Leib, Susan A., and Vollman, John H. "Grief Response of Parents to Neonatal Death and Parent Participation in Deciding Care." *Pediatrics* 62:2 (August 1978), pp. 171-77.

Berger, Merle J. and Goldstein, Donald Peter. "Impaired Reproductive Performance in DES-Exposed Women." *Obstetrics and Gynecology* 55:1 (January 1980), pp. 25-27.

Berkenfield, Janet and Schwartz, Janet B. "Nutrition Intervention in the Community—The 'WIC' Program." *The New England Journal of Medicine* 302:10 (March 6, 1980), pp. 579-81.

Bibring, Grete L. "The Death of an Infant: A Psychiatric Study." *The New England Journal of Medicine* 283:7 (August 13, 1970), pp. 370-71.

Bishop, Edward H. "Genetics in a Clinical Practice." *The Female Patient* 5 (May 1980), pp. 70-73.

The Boston Children's Medical Center. *Pregnancy, Birth, and the Newborn Baby: A Publication for Parents.* New York: Delacorte Press/Seymour Lawrence, 1971.

The Boston Women's Health Book Collective. *Our Bodies, Ourselves: A Book by and for Women.* New York: Simon and Schuster, 1971.

Bottoms, Sidney F., Rosen, Mortimer G., and Sokol, Robert J. "The Increase in the Cesarean Birth Rate." *The New England Journal of Medicine* 302:10 (March 6, 1980), pp. 559-63.

Bradley, Robert A. *Husband-Coached Childbirth.* New York: Harper and Row, 1974.

Brody, Jane E. "Miscarriage: Myths Often Add to Grief." *New York Times*, March 5, 1980.

Brown, Michael H. "Love Canal, U.S.A." *New York Times Magazine*, January 25, 1979, p. 23.

Brydges, Jerauld. " 'Harassment' Irks Paigen at Roswell." *Niagara Gazette*, January 23, 1980.

Buxton, Judith E. and McKay, A. Courtney. "The Effects of a Woman's Unsuccessful Reproductive History on Emotional Stress in a Subsequent Pregnancy." Boston University School of Nursing, August, 1968. Unpublished.

"Caffeine and Birth Defects." March of Dimes Science Information File, September 1980.

Case, Ronna. "When Birth Is Also a Funeral." *The Journal of Pastoral Care* 32:1 (March 1978), pp. 6-21.

Chamberlain, Geoffrey. "Background to Perinatal Health." *The Lancet*, November 17, 1979, pp. 1061-65.

Chase, Helen C. "Perinatal Mortality: Overview and Current Trends." *Clinics in Perinatology* 1:1 (March 1974), pp. 3-15.

Chiswick, Malcolm L. "Antenatal Care and High-Risk Babies." Letter in *British Medical Journal*, February 23, 1980, p. 561.

"Cigarette Smoking and Spontaneous Abortion." *British Medical Journal,* February 4, 1978, p. 259.

Clapp, Diane N. "T Mycoplasm: Its Role in Infertility and Miscarriage." *Resolve,* June 1979, p. 5.

Clyman, Ronald I., Green, Charlotte, Mikkelsen, Cynthia, Rowe, Jane, and Ataide, Linda. "Do Parents Utilize Physician Follow-Up After the Death of Their Newborn?" *Pediatrics* 64:5 (November 1979), pp. 665-67.

Cohen, Marion. "This Is What I Do With Kerin." *Mothering,* Fall 1980, p. 89.

Colman, Arthur D. and Colman, Libby Lee. *Pregnancy: The Psychological Experience.* New York: The Seabury Press, 1971.

Coustan, Donald R. and Garvey, Sheila. *The Baby Team: A Positive Approach to Pregnancy with Diabetes.* St. Louis: Monoject (Division of Sherwood Medical), 1979.

Cullberg, J. "Mental Reactions of Women to Perinatal Death." *Psychosomatic Medicine in Obstetrics and Gynaecology,* 3rd International Congress, London, 1971. Basel, Switz.: Karger, 1972, pp. 326-29.

Culliton, Barbara J. and Waterfall, Wallace K. "Consensus Development—Amniocentesis." *British Medical Journal,* September 22, 1979, pp. 723-24.

Decker, Deborah J. "Grief: In the Valley of the Shadow." *American Journal of Nursing,* March 1978, pp. 416-18.

Dickinson, Emily. *Final Harvest: Emily Dickinson's Poems,* Thomas H. Johnson, ed. Boston: Little, Brown and Company, 1961.

"Drugs and Pregnancy." *The Female Patient* 5 (June 1980), pp. 68-78.

Duff, Raymond S. "Guidelines for Deciding Care of Critically Ill or Dying Patients." *Pediatrics* 64:1 (July 1979), pp. 17-23.

Duff, Raymond S. and Campbell, A.G.M. "Moral and Ethical Dilemmas in the Special-Care Nursery." *The New England Journal of Medicine* 289 (October 25, 1973), pp. 890-94.

Duhring, John L. "Diabetes in Pregnancy." *The Female Patient* 5 (May 1980), pp. 12-18.

Edmiston, Susan and Szekely, Julie. "What We Must Know About Health Hazards in the Workplace." *Redbook,* March 1980, p. 33.

Eisner, Victor, Pratt, Margaret W., Hexter, Alfred, Chabot, Marion Johnson, and Sayal, Naresh. "Improvement in Infant and Perinatal Mortality in the United States, 1965-1973: 1. Priorities for Intervention." *American Journal of Public Health* 68:4 (April 1978), pp. 359-64.

Elia, Andrew D. "The Management of Grief Situations in Obstetrics." *The Boston Medical Quarterly* 10:1 (March 1959).

Eschenbach, David A. "Do Mycoplasmas Cause Infectious Disease?" *Contemporary Obstetrics and Gynecology* 15 (January 1980), pp. 101-7.

Fallaci, Oriana. *Letter to a Child Never Born.* Garden City, N.Y.: Doubleday Anchor Books, 1978.

Fedrick, Jean and Adelstein, Philippa. "Preceding Pregnancy Loss as an Index of Risk of Stillbirth or Neonatal Death in the Present Pregnancy." *Biology of the Neonate* 31 (1977), pp. 84-93.

"Final Mortality Statistics, 1977." National Center for Health Statistics, DHEW

Publication No. (PHS) 79-1120, vol. 28, no. 1, Supplement, May 11, 1979.

"Final Natality Statistics, 1978." National Center for Health Statistics, DHHS Publication No. (PHS) 80-1120, vol. 29, no. 1, Supplement, April 28, 1980.

Friedman, Emanuel A. and Neff, Raymond K. "Hypertension-Hypotension in Pregnancy Correlation with Fetal Outcome." *Journal of the American Medical Association* 239:21 (May 26, 1978), pp. 2249-51.

Frost, Robert. *The Poetry of Robert Frost,* Edward Connery Lathem, ed. New York: Holt, Rinehart and Winston, 1969.

Furman, Erna P. "The Death of a Newborn: Care of the Parents." *Birth and the Family Journal* 5:4 (Winter 1978), pp. 214-18.

Gabbe, Steven G., Mestman, Jorge H., Freeman, Roger K., Goebelsmann, Uwe T., Lowensohn, Richard I., Nochimson, David, Cetrulo, Curtis, and Quilligan, Edward J. "Management and Outcome of Pregnancy in Diabetes Mellitus, Classes B to R." *American Journal of Obstetrics and Gynecology* 129 (1977), pp. 723-32.

Gardiner, Alistair, Clarke, Sir Cyril, Cowen, Jennifer, Finn, Ronald, and McKendrick, Olive M. "Spontaneous Abortion and Fetal Abnormality in Subsequent Pregnancy." *British Medical Journal* 1 (April 22, 1978), pp. 1016-18.

Garite, Thomas J., Freeman, Roger K., Hochleutner, Irene, and Linzey, E. Michael. "Oxytocin Challenge Test: Achieving the Desired Goals." *Obstetrics and Gynecology* 51:5 (May 1978), pp. 614-17.

Garvey, Sheila D. "Diabetic Pregnancy: Questions and Answers for the Diabetes Educator." *The Diabetes Educator,* Fall 1978, pp. 10-23.

Gerber, Irwin, Wiener, Alfred, Kutscher, Austin H., Battin, Delia, Arkin, Arthur, and Goldberg, Ivan K., eds. *Perspectives on Bereavement.* New York: Arno Press, 1979.

Glass, Robert H. and Golbus, Mitchell S. "Habitual Abortion." *Fertility and Sterility* 29:3 (March 1978), pp. 257-64.

Gorer, Geoffrey. *Death, Grief, and Mourning.* Garden City, N.Y.: Doubleday and Company, Inc., 1965.

Grof, Stanislav and Halifax, Joan. *The Human Encounter with Death.* New York: E.P. Dutton, 1977

Grollman, Earl A., ed. *Explaining Death to Children.* Boston: Beacon Press, 1967.

Grollman, Earl A. *Talking About Death: A Dialogue Between Parent and Child.* Boston: Beacon Press, 1976.

Guidelines on Pregnancy and Work. The American College of Obstetricians and Gynecologists/U.S. Department of Health, Education, and Welfare. DHEW (NIOSH) Publication No. 78-118, September 1977.

Hack, Maureen, Fanaroff, Avroy A., and Merkatz, Irwin R. "The Low Birthweight Infant—Evolution of a Changing Outlook." *The New England Journal of Medicine* 301:21 (November 22, 1979), pp. 1162-65.

Hallet, Elizabeth R. "Birth and Grief," *Birth and the Family Journal* 1:4 (1974), pp. 18-22.

Halliday, Henry L., Jones, Paul K., and Jones, Susan L. "Method of Screening Obstetric Patients to Prevent Reproductive Wastage." *Obstetrics and Gynecology* 55:5 (May 1980), pp. 656-61.

Hanson, James W. "Preventing the Fetal Alcohol Syndrome." *The Female Patient,* October 1979, pp. 38-44.

Hardgrove, Carol and Warrick, Louise H. "How Shall We Tell the Children?" *American Journal of Nursing* 74:3 (March 1974), pp. 448-50.

Harlap, S. and Shiono, P.H. "Alcohol, Smoking, and Incidence of Spontaneous Abortions in the First and Second Trimester." *The Lancet,* July 26, 1980, pp.173-80.

Harlap, Susan, Shiono, Patricia, Ramcharan, Savitri, Berendes, Heinz, and Pellegrin, Frederick. "A Prospective Study of Spontaneous Fetal Losses After Induced Abortions." *The New England Journal of Medicine* 301:13 (September 27, 1979), pp. 677-81.

Harris, Rodney. "Maternal Serum Alphafetoprotein in Pregnancy and the Prevention of Birth Defect." *British Medical Journal,* May 17, 1980, pp. 1199-1202.

Herbst, Arthur L. "Coitus and the Fetus." *The New England Journal of Medicine* 301:22 (November 29, 1979), pp. 1235-36.

Hill, Reba M. and Stern, Leo. "Drugs in Pregnancy: Effect on the Fetus and Newborn." *Drugs* 17:3 (March 1979), pp. 182-197.

Hobel, Calvin J. "Better Perinatal Health: U.S.A.," *The Lancet,* January 5, 1980, pp. 31-33.

Hobel, Calvin J., Yonkeles, Lee, and Forsythe, Alan. "Prenatal and Intrapartum High Risk Screening: II. Risk Factors Reassessed." *American Journal of Obstetrics and Gynecology* 135 (December 15, 1979), pp. 1051-56.

Hughes-Tremper, Sherron and Nelson, Barbara. "On the Death of an Infant." Information booklet, Lutheran General Hospital, Park Ridge, Ill.

Iams, Jay D. and Rayburn, Willam F. "Drug Use During Pregnancy. Part II. Drug Effects on the Fetus." *Perinatal Press* 4:9 (October 1980), pp. 131-136.

Ishida, Yasuo. "How to Deal with Grief in Childbirth." *The Female Patient* 5 (May 1980), p. 74

Isler, Charlotte. "Infecton: Constant Threat to Perinatal Life." *RN* 38:8 (August 1975), pp. 23-29

Johnson, Joan Marie. "Stillbirth—A Personal Experience." *American Journal of Nursing* 72:9 (September 1972), pp.1595-96.

Jouppila, Pentti. "Pregnancy-Specific B-Glycoprotein in Complication of Early Pregnancy." *The Lancet,* March 29, 1980, pp. 667-68.

Kamien, Marcia. "The Death of a New Baby: The Grief No One Wants to Talk About." *Glamour,* May 1979, pp.187-89.

Kaplan, Louise J. *Oneness and Separateness: From Infant to Individual.* New York: Simon and Schuster, 1978.

Keirse, M.J.N.C., Rush, R.W., Anderson, A.B.M., and Turnbull, A.C. "Risk of Pre-Term Delivery in Patients With Previous Pre-Term Delivery and/or Abortion." *British Journal of Obstetrics and Gynaecology* 85:2 (February 1978), pp. 81-85

Kelly, Marguerite and Parsons, Elia. *The Mother's Almanac.* Garden City, N.Y.: Doubleday and Company, Inc., 1975.

Kennell, John H., Slyter, Howard, and Klaus, Marshall H. "The Mourning Response of Parents to the Death of a Newborn Infant." *The New England Journal of Medicine* 283:7 (August 13, 1970), pp. 344-49.

Kent, Deryck R., and Goldstein, Arthur I. "Prostaglandin E2 Induction of Labor for Fetal Demise." *Obstetrics and Gynecology* 48:4 (October 1976), pp. 475-78.

Klaus, Marshall H. and Fanaroff, Avery A. *Care of the High-Risk Neonate.* Philadelphia: W. B. Saunders Company, 1973.

Klaus, Marshall H. and Kennell, John H. *Maternal-Infant Bonding: The Impact of Early Separation or Loss on Family Development.* St. Louis: The C.V. Mosby Company, 1976.

Klemesrud, Judy. "Helping Couples Cope with the Loss of an Infant." *New York Times,* May 29, 1978.

Kleiman, Dena. "Anguished Search to Cure Infertility." *New York Times Magazine,* December 16, 1979, p. 38.

Kliman, Ann S. *Crisis: Psychological First Aid for Recovery and Growth.* New York: Holt, Rinehart and Winston, 1978.

Kliman, Gilbert W. *Psychological Emergencies of Childhood.* New York: Grune and Stratton, 1968.

Kliman, Gilbert W. and Rosenfeld, Albert. *Responsible Parenthood: The Child's Psyche Through the Six-Year Pregnancy.* New York: Holt, Rinehart and Winston, 1980.

Kline, Jennie, Stein, Zena, Strobino, Barbara, Susser, Mervyn, and Warburton, Dorothy. "Surveillance of Spontaneous Abortions: Power in Environmental Monitoring." *American Journal of Epidemiology* 106:5 (1977), pp. 345-50.

Kline, Jennie, Stein, Zena, Susser, Mervyn, and Warburton, Dorothy. "Smoking: A Risk Factor for Spontaneous Abortion." *The New England Journal of Medicine* 297 (1977), p. 793.

Knapp, Ronald J. and Peppers, Larry G. "Doctor-Patient Relationships in Fetal/Infant Death Encounters." *Journal of Medical Education* 54 (October 1979), pp. 775-80.

Kolata, Gina Bari. "Behavioral Teratology: Birth Defects of the Mind." *Science* 202 (November 17, 1978), pp. 732-34.

———. "Prenatal Diagnosis of Neural Tube Defects." *Science* 209 (September 12, 1980), pp. 1216-18.

Kotzwinkle, William. *Swimmer in the Secret Sea.* New York: Avon Books, 1975.

Krell, Robert and Rabkin, Leslie. "The Effects of Sibling Death on the Surviving Child: A Family Perspective." *Family Process* 18 (December 1979), pp. 471-77.

Kübler-Ross, Elisabeth. *On Death and Dying.* New York: Macmillan Publishing Co., Inc., 1969.

Lawrence, K.M., James, Nanci, Miller, Mary, Campbell, H. "Increased Risk of Recurrence of Pregnancies Complicated by Fetal Neural Tube Defects in Mothers Receiving Poor Diets, and Possible Benefit of Dietary Counseling." *British Medical Journal* 281 (December 13, 1980), pp. 1592-94.

Levinson, Gershon and Shnider, Sol M. "Catecholamines: The Effects of Maternal Fear and Its Treatment on Uterine Function and Circulation." *Birth and the Family Journal* 6:3 (Fall 1979), pp. 167-74.

Lewis, C. S. *A Grief Observed.* New York: The Seabury Press, 1961.

Lewis, Emanuel. "The Management of Stillbirth: Coping with an Unreality." *The Lancet,* September 18, 1976, pp. 619-20.

Lindemann, Erich. "Symptomatology and Management of Acute Grief." *American Journal of Psychiatry* 101 (September 1944), pp. 141-48.

Longo, Lawrence D. "Environmental Pollution and Pregnancy: Risks and Uncertainties for the Fetus and Infant." *American Journal of Obstetrics and Gynecology* 137:2 (May 15, 1980), pp. 162-73.

The Loss of Your Baby. Booklet for parents produced by The [British] Health Education Council in conjunction with The National Association for Mental Health and The National Stillbirth Study Group.

Lubchenco, Lula O. *The High Risk Infant.* Philadelphia: W.B. Saunders Company, 1976.

Lumley, Judith and Bell, Robin. "Stress and Premature Labour." *British Medical Journal,* November 10, 1979, p. 1222.

MacCarthy, Dermod. "The Repercussions of the Death of a Child." *Proceedings of the Royal Society of Medicine* 62 (June 1969), pp. 553-54.

Macholi, Libby. "Environmental Hazards: What They'll Mean to Your Patients in the 1980's." *Contemporary Obstetrics and Gynecology* 15 (January 1980), pp. 22-43.

MacVicar, John and Kerr, Margaret. "Maternal Disease, Infection, Trauma, Rhesus Isoimmunisation." *The Lancet,* December 15, 1979, pp. 1284-87.

Management of Diabetes Mellitus in Pregnancy. American College of Obstetricians and Gynecologists, Technical Bulletin #48, April 1978.

Manniello, Robert L. and Farrell, Philip M. "Analysis of United States Neonatal Mortality Statistics from 1968 to 1974, with Specific Reference to Changing Trends in Major Causalities." *American Journal of Obstetrics and Gynecology* 129 (November 15, 1977), pp. 667-74.

Mazor, Miriam D. "Barren Couples." *Psychology Today,* May 1979, pp. 102-12.

McCormack, Michael K. "Medical Genetics and Family Practice." *American Family Physician* 20:3 (September 1979), pp. 142-54.

Menning, Barbara Eck. *Infertility: A Guide for the Childless Couple.* Englewood Cliffs, N.J.: Prentice-Hall, Inc., 1977.

Millis, James B. "Complications of Early Pregnancy." *Perinatal Care* 2:4 (April 1978), pp. 26-29.

Mills, Gretchen Curtis. "Books to Help Children Understand Death." *American Journal of Nursing,* February 1979, pp. 291-95.

Morrison, I. and Olsen, J. "Perinatal Mortality and Antepartum Risk Scoring." *Obstetrics and Gynecology* 53:3 (March 1979), pp. 362-66.

Moriarty, Irene. "Mourning the Death of an Infant: The Sibling's Story." *The Journal of Pastoral Care* 32:1 (March 1978), pp.22-33.

Myles, Margaret F. *Textbook for Midwives: With Modern Concepts of Obstetrics and Neonatal Care.* 8th ed., Edinburgh, Scotl.: Churchill Livingstone, 1975.

Naeye, Richard L. "Abruptio Placentae and Placenta Previa: Frequency, Perinatal Mortality, and Cigarette Smoking," *Obstetrics and Gynecology* 55:6 (June 1980), pp. 701-4.

————. "Causes and Consequences of Placental Growth Retardation." *The Journal of the American Medical Association* 239:12 (March 20, 1978), pp. 1145-47.

————. "Causes of Perinatal Mortality in the U.S. Collaborative Perinatal Project." *The Journal of the American Medical Association* 238 (1977), pp. 228-29.

————. "Coitus and Associated Amniotic-Fluid Infections." *The New England Journal of Medicine* 301:22 (November 29, 1979), pp. 1198-1200.

————. "Effects of Maternal Cigarette Smoking on the Fetus and Placenta." *British Journal of Obstetrics and Gynaecology* 85 (1978), pp. 732-37.

Naeye, Richard L. and Blanc, William A. "Relation of Poverty and Race to Antenatal Infection." *The New England Journal of Medicine*, 283:11 (September 10, 1970), pp. 555-59.

Naeye, Richard L., Harkness, William L., and Utts, Jessica. "Abruptio Placentae and Perinatal Death: A Prospective Study." *American Journal of Obstetrics and Gynecology* 128 (August 1, 1977), pp. 740-46.

Naeye, Richard L. and Peters, Ellen C. "Causes and Consequences of Premature Rupture of Fetal Membranes." *The Lancet*, January 26, 1980, pp. 192-94.

Nahmias, André J. "The TORCH Complex." *Hospital Practice*, May 1974, pp. 65-72

Newton, Richard W., Webster, Pat A.C., Binu, P.S., Maskrey, Neal, and Phillips, A.B. "Psychosocial Stress in Pregnancy and Its Relation to the Onset of Premature Labour." *British Medical Journal*, August 18, 1979, pp. 411-13.

Niswander, Kenneth R. and Gordon, Myron. *The Women and Their Pregnancies: The Collaborative Perinatal Study of the National Institute of Neurologial Diseases and Stroke.* Philadelphia: W.B. Saunders Company, 1972

Nursing Care Following a Stillbirth or a Neonatal Death. Booth Maternity Center Guidelines, revised December 1978.

Opirhory, Gloria J. "Counseling the Parents of a Critically Ill Newborn." *Journal of Obstetric, Gynecologic, and Neonatal Nursing*, May/June 1979, pp. 179-82.

"Origin of Maternal Serum AFP." *The Lancet*, November 10, 1979, pp. 999-1000.

Paigen, Beverly. "Health Hazards at Love Canal." Testimony presented to the House Subcommittee on Oversight and Investigations, March 21, 1979.

Parkes, Colin Murray. *Bereavement: Studies of Grief in Adult Life.* New York: International Universities Press, Inc., 1972.

Potter, Edith Louise and Craig, John M. *Pathology of the Fetus and the Infant.* 3rd ed., Chicago: Year Book Medical Publishers, Inc., 1975.

Powledge, Tabitha M. and Fletcher, John. "Guidelines for the Ethical, Social, and Legal Issues in Prenatal Diagnosis." A report from the Genetics Research Group of the Hastings Center, Institute of Society, Ethics, and the Life Sciences. *The New England Journal of Medicine* 300 (1979), pp. 168-72.

Poznanski, Elva Orlow. "The 'Replacement Child': A Saga of Unresolved Parental Grief." *The Journal of Pediatrics* 81:6 (December 1972), pp. 1190-93.

"Pregnancy in the Underweight Woman." *British Medical Journal*, May 10, 1980, p. 1154.

Pregnancy Metabolism, Diabetes and the Fetus. Ciba Foundation Symposium 63. Amsterdam: Excerpta Medica, 1979.

"Quality Not Quantity in Babies." *British Medical Journal*, February 9, 1980, p. 347.

Ritchie, Knox and McClore, Garth. "Prematurity." *The Lancet*, December 8, 1979, pp. 1227-28.

Rowe, Jane, Clyman, Ronald, Green, Charlotte, Mikkelsen, Cynthia, Haight, Jeanette, and Ataide, Linda. "Follow-Up of Families Who Experience a Perinatal Death." *Pediatrics* 62:2 (August 1978), pp. 166-70.

Rushton, D.I. "Simplified Classification of Spontaneous Abortions." *Journal of Medical Genetics* 15 (1978), pp. 1-9.

Rutland, Andrew and Ballard, Charles. "Vaginal Prostaglandin E2 for Missed Abortion and Intrauterine Fetal Death." *American Journal of Obstetrics and Gynecology* 128:5 (1977), pp. 503-5.

Sandler, Bernard. "Emotional Stress and Infertility." *Journal of Psychosomatic Research* 12 (1968), pp. 51-59.

Schiff, Harriet Sarnoff. *The Bereaved Parent.* Harmondsworth, Middlesex, Engl.: Penguin Books, 1977.

Schneider, Jan. "Repeated Pregnancy Loss." *Clinical Obstetrics and Gynecology,* March 1973, pp. 120-33.

Schneider, Kathy D. and Daniel, Janet S. "Dealing with Perinatal Death: Professionals and Parents Together." *Perinatal Press* 3:7 (July/August 1979), pp. 101-5.

Schoenbaum, Stephen C., Monson, Richard R., Stubblefield, Phillip G., Darney, Philip D., and Ryan, Kenneth J. "Outcome of the Delivery Following an Induced or Spontaneous Abortion." *American Journal of Obstetrics and Gynecology* 136 (January 1, 1980), pp. 19-24.

Scrimgeour, J.B. and Cockburn, F. "Congenital Abnormalities." *The Lancet,* December 22/29, 1979, pp. 1349-52.

Scupholme, Anne. "Who Helps? Coping with the Unexpected Outcomes of Pregnancy." *Journal of Obstetric, Gynecologic, and Neonatal Nursing,* July/August 1978, pp. 36-39.

Seitz, Pauline M. and Warrick, Louise H. "Perinatal Death: The Grieving Mother." *American Journal of Nursing* 74:11 (November 1974), pp. 2028-33.

Sheer, Barbara Lee. "Help for Parents in a Difficult Job—Broaching the Subject of Death." *American Journal of Maternal and Child Nursing,* September /October 1977, pp. 320-24.

Shribman, David. "House Study Asks Canal Evacuation." *Buffalo Evening News,* October 14, 1979.

Simpson, Joe Leigh. "Repeated Suboptimal Pregnancy Outcome." Paper presented at the March of Dimes Birth Defects Conference, June 10, 1980.

Slade, Margot. "Infant Death and Parental Grief: Debunking the Old Notions." *New York Times,* September 13, 1980.

Snyder, Dona J. "The High-Risk Mother Viewed in Relation to a Holistic Model of the Childbearing Experience." *Journal of Obstetric, Gynecologic, and Neonatal Nursing,* May/June 1979, pp. 164-70.

Sobel, Dana. "Simple Test Could Screen All Expectant Mothers." *New York Times,* January 13, 1981.

Speck, William T. "Commentary: The Tragedy of Stillbirth." *The Journal of Pediatrics* 93:5 (November 1978), pp. 869-70.

Speroff, Leon, Glass, Robert, and Kase, Nathan. *Clinical Gynecologic Endocrinology and Infertility.* Baltimore: The Williams and Wilkins Company, 1973.

Stack, Jack M. "Spontaneous Abortion and Grieving," *American Family Physician* 21:5 (May 1980), pp. 99-102.

Storlie, Frances J. "Burnout: The Elaboration of a Concept." *American Journal of Nursing,* December 1979, pp. 2108-11.

Strobino, Barbara R., Kline, Jennie, and Stein, Zena. "Chemical and Physical Exposures of Parents: Effects on Human Reproduction and Offspring." *Journal of Early Human Development* 1:4 (February 1978), pp. 371-99.

Tho, Phung Thi, Byrd, J. Rogers, and McDonough, Paul G. "Etiologies and Subsequent Reproductive Performance of 100 Couples with Recurrent Abortion." *Fertility and Sterility* 32:4 (October 1979), pp. 389-94.

Thom, Margaret H., Chan, K.K., and Studd, J.W.W. "Outcome of Normal and Dysfunctional Labor in Different Racial Groups." *American Journal of Obstetrics and Gynecology* 135 (October 15, 1979), pp. 495-98.

Thomas, Lewis. "Dying As Failure," *Annals of the American Academy of Political and Social Science* 447 (January 1980), p. 1.

Thompson, Theodore R. and Reynolds, John W. "The Result of Intensive Care Therapy for Neonates." *Journal of Perinatal Medicine* 5 (1977), pp. 57-99.

Thullen, James D. "When You Can't Cure, Care." *P/N*, November/December 1977, pp. 31-46.

Tichy, Anna M. and Chong, Dianne. "Placental Function and Its Role in Toxemia." *American Journal of Maternal and Child Nursing*, March/April 1979, pp. 84-95.

"Vitamins, Neural-Tube Defects, and Ethics Committees." *The Lancet*, May 17, 1980, pp. 1061-62.

Wallace, Helen M. "Status of Infant and Perinatal Morbidity and Mortality: A Review of the Literature." *Public Health Reports* 93:4 (July-August 1978), pp. 386-93.

Warburton, Dorothy, Kline, Jennie, Stein, Zena, and Susser, Mervyn. "Monosomy X: A Chromosomal Anomaly Associated with Young Maternal Age." *The Lancet*, January 26, 1980, pp. 167-69.

Warburton, Dorothy, Susser, Mervyn, Stein, Zena, and Kline, Jennie. "Genetic and Epidemiologic Investigation of Spontaneous Abortion: Relevance to Clinical Practice." *Birth Defects: Original Article Series* 15:5A, pp. 127-36.

Warshaw, Joseph. "Newborn Intensive Care: The First 20 Years in Perspective." *Hospital Practice*, October 1980, pp. 14-15.

Weiner, Stuart, Librizzi, Ronald J., and Bolognese, Ronald J. "Postdate Pregnancy: Its Risks and Management." *Contemporary Obstetrics and Gynecology* 14 (October 1979), pp. 133-47.

Welch, Mary Scott and Herrmann, Dorothy. "Why Miscarriage Is So Misunderstood: New Medical and Emotional Findings. . . ." *Ms.*, February 1980, pp. 14-22.

Welt, Selman I. and Crenshaw, M. Carlyle, Jr. "Concurrent Hypertension and Pregnancy." *Clinical Obstetrics and Gynecology* 21:3 (September 1978), pp. 619-46.

Willson, J. Robert, Beecham, Clayton T., and Carrington, Elsie Reid. *Obstetrics and Gynecology*. 4th ed., St. Louis: The C.V. Mosby Company, 1971.

Wilson, Robert W. and Schifrin, Barry S. "Is Any Pregnancy Low Risk?" *Obstetrics and Gynecology* 55:5 (May 1980), pp. 653-55.

Wolff, John R., Nielson, Paul E., and Schiller, Patricia. "The Emotional Reaction to a Stillbirth." *American Journal of Obstetrics and Gynecology* 108:1 (September 1, 1970), pp. 73-77.

Worlow, Dorothy. "What Do You Say When the Baby Is Stillborn?" *RN*, July 1980.

Worton, Ronald G. "Chromosome Abnormalities: A Major Cause of Birth Defects, Stillbirth, and Spontaneous Abortion." *Canadian Medical Association Journal* 117 (October 22, 1977), pp. 849-51.

Wyss, Mary. "Patterns of Grief in a Mother Experiencing Newborn Death." Pamphlet prepared for A.M.E.N.D. (Aiding a Mother Experiencing Neo-Natal Death), St. Louis, Missouri.

Yates, Susan A. "Stillbirth—What a Staff Can Do." *American Journal of Nursing* 72:9 (September 1972), pp. 1592-94.

Index

171

About the Author

NANCY BEREZIN is a medical writer and editor specializing in obstetrics/gynecology and pediatrics. In addition to monographs and magazine articles, her published works include *The Gentle Birth Book: A Practical Guide to Leboyer Family-Centered Delivery*.